Breakout

Breakout

THE GOOD DAUGHTER   Ginny Collins

PYG
        Rose Condo

TO FORGIVE, DIVÍNE
                Joseph Aragon

CT
David Ferber

SHADES OF BROWN   Primrose Madayag Knazan

Edited by Brian Drader

with an Introduction by RORY RUNNELLS

Breakout
first published 2004 by
Scirocco Drama
An imprint of J. Gordon Shillingford Publishing Inc.
© 2004 the Authors

Scirocco Drama Editor: Glenda MacFarlane
Cover design by Terry Gallagher/Doowah Design Inc.
Printed and bound in Canada

We acknowledge the financial support of The Canada Council for the Arts
and the Manitoba Arts Council for our publishing program.

Canadian Cataloguing in Publication Data

Breakout/edited by Brian Drader.

Contents: The good daughter/Ginny Collins—Shades of brown/Primrose Madayag
Knazan—To forgive, divine/Joseph Aragon—Pyg/Rose Condo—PACT/David
Ferber.

ISBN 0-920486-63-0

1. Canadian drama (English)—21st century. I. Drader, Brian, 1960–

PS8315.B74 2004   C812'.608   C2004-902025-0

J. Gordon Shillingford Publishing
P.O. Box 86, RPO Corydon Avenue, Winnipeg, MB Canada R3M 3S3

Table of Contents

Foreword

In 2000, my introduction to a collection of plays celebrating the Manitoba Association of Playwrights twentieth anniversary, entitled *A MAP of the Senses*, concluded:

> Fortunately, more Manitoba plays are being published, and we wait for young energetic writers…to form the core of the next collection. No one volume can contain as complex, unruly and diverse body of work produced here over the past twenty years. In this one, we have tried. Meanwhile, the work proceeds.

Well, it's four years on, the work has proceeded, and here is a collection, selected by Brian Drader, by some of those young, energetic writers who have sprung up in the time since as we head towards our 25th Anniversary in the fall of 2004. As with the previous one, this collection can't pretend to contain the diverse work produced in the past few years by Manitoba's young playwrights, loosely defined by us as between eighteen and twenty-eight (okay, we can push it to thirty if you like); maybe young, emerging is the better description. It is, actually, and that's why MAP and Prairie Theatre Exchange started the Young Emerging Playwrights Program in 2001: to provide a focus for the emerging playwrights who come from disparate places: a high school playwriting competition, or first production(for which some far sighted high schools deserve credit in doing original plays), or the PlayBlitz for senior high school playwrights, or that first Fringe production, or even the odd desire to write for the theatre, which hardly seems the place the young might go to create, film and video being stridently dominant in the culture they live in. In fact, what is encouraging, even wonderful in its way, is that the young playwrights we have encountered over the past few years don't regard theatre as a way station on the road to their first feature film, but integral to their expression as striving, emerging artists.

I know Brian had difficulty choosing from the entries; who wouldn't? This selection of playwrights under thirty, however, who have come up in precisely the ways listed above is as representative as any of the many themes, styles, dramatic sophistication, and sheer bountiful exuberance which we see in the growing number of plays by our emerging young playwrights. We tend to forget that we are now into at least a third generation of playwrights in Canada, and at least a second in Manitoba, not forgetting those who cried in the wilderness before, say, 1980 when the movement, if it can be grandly called that, towards an indigenous local playwriting made its appearance.

Here isn't the place to discuss that period again (that was done in the introduction to *A MAP of the Senses*) though it was an exciting one, the first boom in Manitoba playwriting, or how it declined in some ways in the nineties, but what should be mentioned is the impact of the Fringe on the new generation of playwrights, and the solidifying of programs of support for playwrights. What has that done to and for this new generation?

What having a system of ongoing support through MAP has meant is that playwrights don't feel isolated; there is a place which pays the attention needed. The new playwrights are much more a community, and are comfortable in that community, perhaps, than the previous one, which struggled to find and hold community in their work. The new playwrights expect support, not out of arrogance or right, but because they know theatre is important, and the creation of indigenous plays is the lifeblood of any important theatre. That belief has led our organization to a better understanding of how to work with playwrights; we embrace the challenge, and our work grows.

While they develop their work here, they also produce, mainly at the Fringe. The Fringe's time constraints have made the new playwrights sharper than the previous generation in honing their material, while, at the same time, perhaps, boxing them into writing plays with somewhat less ambition and outlook. Still the new playwrights have come to dominate the loose, improvisational style of the Fringe in the best way, while still dealing with some important issues, and attempting new forms. Often there being few other places to go for production (that's another story needing telling; the new generation would love productions at the main theatres—they just don't pine waiting for them), the Fringe has provided the new playwrights with an opportunity, and they have taken to it as 'their' theatre. Also, they are learning fast, and defying the sixty/seventy minute "rule" of a Fringe play to learn to write what is really needed which, simply, more time often demands. And anything still goes, not in the careless sense of wanting to shock, but in needing to express what underlies their lives. Brian Drader has smartly written about each play, but, young or not, this generation is in line with its predecessors, I think, in writing about their Winnipeg with a new take. It is still a world of urban blues, political edge, new immigration remaking the streets, a certain surreal loneliness which our famous isolation as a winter Prairie city invites. Now, perhaps, the world is a harsher place, but Brian is right in sensing an optimism and embrace of the contradictions in the life of this faded, yet pulsating, city. Attention will be paid, to paraphrase *Death of a Salesman*, and we know these playwrights and colleagues will breakout to a rich theatrical life. They want it, and our theatres need it.

Rory Runnells
March, 2004

Introduction

I first started working with young writers in the early 90s. The program was called PlayBlitz, sponsored by Prairie Theatre Exchange in Winnipeg, and was geared towards assisting six high school playwrights in the development of their plays over the course of seven months. I remember our very first meeting—I'm sure I was more nervous that any of them. I'd written four plays at that point in my career, and I was being asked to shepherd these six young minds through the immensely personal and complicated and frustrating and joyous process of writing a play. I hadn't a clue what I was doing.

I made it through that first meeting, and went on to have one of the most influential and rewarding experiences of my life. I was taught so much that year, as I tried desperately to communicate to them what I thought I knew. I was reminded of how vulnerable and passionate and pure and sometimes innocent a young voice can be, and have attempted to preserve that vulnerability and passion and purity (and a little bit of that innocence) in my own voice ever since. Those six young writers also taught me to break all the silly, unnecessary and often damaging "rules" that I'd somehow foolishly collected in my early career to shore up and protect my own work. They didn't know any of these rules. No one had harnessed them with a doctrine of writing rights and wrongs. In their innocence, they were able to explore the craft of playwrighting in a way that I had long ago forgotten. What a lovely and valuable lesson that was for me.

After ten years and sixty young playwrights, PlayBlitz morphed into the Young Emerging Playwrights Program (YEPP), co-sponsored by Prairie Theatre Exchange and the Manitoba Association of Playwrights. YEPP is presently in its third year. The structure of the program is the same, as is the process. Instead of high school students, the YEPP playwrights are in their late teens and twenties, and come to the program with a little more life experience, and with a play or two under their belts. I'm now middle-aged, with a few more plays under my belt as well. Nothing else has changed. The young voices are still vulnerable and passionate and pure and sometimes innocent, all the "rules" are still being broken with brilliantly unaware verve and abandonment, and I'm still learning far more from them that they are from me.

Of the five playwrights in this anthology, three were either participants in the PlayBlitz or the YEPP program. The other two are quickly establishing themselves amongst the next generation of Manitoba playwrights. They all share what I believe is the only thing that can't be taught to a writer. We all have imaginations, an ability to suspend our disbelief, to create a world that didn't exist before we put pen to paper, and if we have the desire (and patience), we can all be taught the craft of writing. What can't be taught is courage, and above all it takes courage to write.

Joseph Aragon's *To Forgive, Divine* challenges the Christian principle of redemption as it affects a mother and daughter trying to find their way back to each other; Primrose Madayag Knazan's *Shades of Brown* uses the Filipino immigration experience to explore cultural assumptions, interracial dating, racism, and that elusive sense of belonging that we call 'home'; Ginny Collin's *The Good Daughter* dives deep into the delicious genre of black comedy, exposing a highly dysfunctional family of three women running rum on the prairies; David Ferber's *PACT* looks at teenage suicide with a darkly hilarious, disturbing, and ultimately hopeful effect; and Rose Condo's *pyg* tells the funny and touching story of one woman's struggle with loneliness and the relentlessly impossible ideals our culture's media imposes on us.

These five young playwrights have courage in abundance; the courage to look at themselves, the courage to say what they think, and the courage to explore how they feel. Above all, they have the courage to share that with an audience, and with you, the reader. I so admire them for that, and learn from it, and draw my own courage from it.

I'd like very much to thank my friend Kathy Clune for her invaluable contribution to this anthology. She has for years been my "shadow" dramaturge, reading all my plays and correcting all my spelling mistakes (I have always been and continue to be a horrible speller, although I am improving under her tutelage), and lending me her unerring sense of character and story. She was a huge assist in putting together this anthology. I'd also like to thank Gordon Shillingford for giving me this opportunity.

Working with these five young playwrights has been a joy and an education. They are our future, and I'm thrilled to be a part of it.

Brian Drader
March, 2004

The Good Daughter

Ginny Collins

Characters

LAUREL: 36, thin, trashy, vulgar.

JANICE: her sister, 32, somewhat overweight, dumpy.

MS. QUINN: their mother, old, chubby, frail, in a wheelchair, carries around a large stick with a clamp at the end for grabbing things.

JERRY
HADDOCK: police officer, 37, unattractive, awkward, dimwitted.

Set

1930s. Two separate rooms in a small cabin. The kitchen has a simple wooden table in the middle of the room with three wooden chairs, a rocking chair and counters along the back with drawers and a stove. There are boxes in the corner. Along the back wall are shelves with various bottles, statues and tins. Ms. Quinn's room is next to the kitchen. The bed is in the middle of the room. On the side of the bed closest to the door there is a shelf with various ornaments on it. On the other side there is a night table.

The play itself takes place in the small town of Wadena, Saskatchewan.

Scene 1

When the lights come up on the kitchen, MS. QUINN is in her old wooden wheelchair. She is hunched and has a miserable look on her face. She suddenly wheels her chair around and goes over to the counter. She takes her clamper and grabs a bottle of pills that are lying on the bottom shelf. She moves them to the top shelf. She then wheels herself over to the table once again. She checks her watch. Footsteps are heard from outside and the doorknob turns. MS. QUINN quickly slumps in her chair and closes her eyes as if she has been sleeping.

LAUREL emerges into the house and begins to take off her coat. She looks into the kitchen, sees that her mother is sleeping and slams the door behind her with a loud bang.

MS. QUINN: *(Startled.)* Good Jesus!

LAUREL: Awwww. Were ya sleepin' Ma?

MS. QUINN: Yes.

LAUREL: Well, that's too bad. I feel awful bad about it, wakin' you up.

MS. QUINN: Yes.

LAUREL takes something out of the refrigerator, sits down at the table and begins to eat quickly. MS. QUINN stares straight ahead and frowns.

LAUREL: Funny thing there Ma.

MS. QUINN: Yes.

LAUREL: I was walkin' to the grocery store in town and I passed Constable Baker. He waved to me, 'cause me and him always exchange polite conversation, and he said "Hey there Laurel, where ya off to?" and I said, "Oh just the grocery store Constable Baker." And then he calls back "Oh well then, you have a good day and you make sure you say hello to your old Ma and you ask her how she's doin' for me." I thought that was real nice of him. He sure does like us.

MS. QUINN: Very nice of him.

LAUREL: Sure was Ma, sure was.

              Pause, the two peer at each other for a few moments.

              Oh! I almost forgot.

MS. QUINN: What's that?

LAUREL: When I got to the tin shop do ya know what Mr. Hammond said? He said that my pay would have to be delayed for another week. Can you believe that Ma? Another week. But I said to him, I said "That's alright then Mr. Hammond, I have lots of debts and all, but if you can't afford it this week, then I guess that's alright. Plus I have a nice old Ma that helps me out when I'm in real need."

MS. QUINN: That was nice of you, to be so understanding.

LAUREL: Ya.

              Pause.

MS. QUINN: Laurel?

LAUREL: *(Quickly.)* Yes Ma?

MS. QUINN: It seems that it's time for me to take my pills Laurel.

LAUREL: Is it Ma?

MS. QUINN: Yes, and it seems that once again you have placed my pills on the very top shelf where I cannot possibly reach them.

LAUREL: Huh? No Ma, it wasn't me, I never put them up there, it must have been Janice—

MS. QUINN: Laurel, I distinctly remember that you were the last one to give me my pills. I think sometimes that you put them up there on that top shelf on purpose.

LAUREL: No Ma I never—

MS. QUINN: Go and fetch them now.

Pause. LAUREL gets up from her place at the table and drags a chair over to the shelves. She gets out a wooden spoon and uses it to reach to the top shelf for the bottle of pills. She gets them down and brings them to her mother along with her pill container.

LAUREL: There you are.

She carefully lays out the articles in front of her mother.

LAUREL sits back down in her place and watches her mother. MS. QUINN very slowly opens each container and puts her pills in the according slots. She does this painfully slowly so that LAUREL is forced to stay there and watch. After she is done she hands the pills back to LAUREL and she hurriedly places them on the lowest shelf.

LAUREL: I was just about to ask you Ma.

MS. QUINN: Yes.

LAUREL: I was just about to ask you if I could borrow a bit of money. Just until next week when Mr. Hammond can pay me.

MS.QUINN: Why yes then Laurel, why didn't ya just ask me? I am always as happy as a clam to lend money to my two self-sufficient daughters, God love 'em. I really don't feel that I do enough, providing them with a roof over their heads and food to eat when they're at the ever so young age of 30 something. Would you perhaps like the clothes off my back then? Or do ya think you could leave an old woman alone, just for once. Because all you'll be gettin' will be the steam off my pee!

She slams her hands down on the table and LAUREL jumps.

MS. QUINN wheels herself out of the room. LAUREL is left standing in the room glaring after her mother. She stays there for a moment and then takes her dinner from the table and throws it in the garbage.

Just then, a drunken version of "Amazing Grace" is heard from outside and LAUREL goes over to the window and peers outside.

LAUREL: *(Sighs.)* Fuck.

She goes over to the door and opens it wide. JANICE enters just as she is finishing the last line of her song. She is holding a bible in one hand and a bottle of rum in the other. She then looks around the room slowly and her eyes finally rest on LAUREL.

JANICE: Well, hello there!

LAUREL: And hello to you, ya fat old fuck. *(She slams the door.)*

JANICE: You should watch your language you know, *(She whispers and points to the ceiling.)* ya never know who is listenin'.

LAUREL: You're drunk as a sailor and you're talkin' to me about language. *(She looks behind her toward where her mother exited.)* Ma's awake right now you know, and if she catches you like this we're both in for it Janice.

Just then MS. QUINN's squeaky wheelchair is heard coming back into the room. LAUREL quickly looks

around then shoves JANICE out the door and leans
against it. MS. QUINN enters the room.

MS. QUINN: What was all that noise I heard?

LAUREL: Was nothin'.

MS. QUINN: I was sure I heard Jan's voice in here.

LAUREL: Ohh, you must have been mistaken.

MS. QUINN: *(She glares at LAUREL.)* You're sure it was nothin'?

LAUREL: Yes ma'am.

Just as MS. QUINN turns to leave, JANICE knocks
on the door. She stops and turns.

MS. QUINN: Well—

LAUREL: Well what?

MS. QUINN: Was that not the door I just heard knocking?

LAUREL: The door? This door? No I really don't think so.

JANICE knocks once again, louder.

MS. QUINN: Are you going to answer that?

Pause.

LAUREL: No.

MS. QUINN: No?

LAUREL: No, I really wouldn't. You never know who could
               be knocking at this time of ni-

MS. QUINN: *(Interrupts.)* Answer the door Laurel.

Pause. She answers the door.

LAUREL: Jan!

She quickly grabs JANICE and pulls her into the
house. She takes her bottle of rum and hides it behind

her back. She then pushes JANICE into a kitchen chair.

Well there. Home all safe and sound. You best be gettin' off to bed then there Ma.

MS. QUINN stares at them for a while. And then wheels slowly off to bed.

G' night then!

LAUREL watches her leave the room and listens for her to close her bedroom door. She turns to JANICE.

What the hell is wrong with you? You know that all she needs is an excuse. She'll be on us like a wolf on a rabbit.

JANICE: Oh God, I'm sorry Laurel.

She is nearly in tears.

LAUREL: You better watch it. You just better watch.

JANICE: Oh forgive me.

LAUREL: It really doesn't matter if I forgive you or not Jan. It's Ma you'll have to answer to.

JANICE: You never forgive me. Oh God. *(She opens her bible and frantically flips through it. She reads from the bible.)* "You will not let your Holy One see decay. For when David had served God's purpose in his own generation, he fell asleep; he was buried with his father and his body decayed...

LAUREL: Oh good grief.

As she reads this quote she leans farther and farther into the bible until she is resting her face on the bible and she falls asleep face first in it.

JANICE: *(Speaking over LAUREL.)* But the one whom God raised from the dead did not see decay! Therefore, my brothers, I want you to know that through Jesus the forgiveness of sins is proclaimed to you."

JANICE is asleep.

LAUREL: Holy shit.

LAUREL takes JANICE's bottle of rum and heads off toward her own bedroom.

Scene 2

Morning. Lights come up on JANICE who is still sleeping face first in her bible. She is snoring. There is a knock on the door. The person knocks several times and JANICE goes on sleeping. The person finally tries the door and upon finding it unlocked comes into the kitchen. It is JERRY, one of the town's police officers. He is in his police uniform. JERRY sees that JANICE is sleeping on the table and stands there awkwardly for a few moments. He fixes his hair.

JERRY: S'cuse me. *(Pause, he shakes JANICE's shoulder.)* Janice? *(Pause.)* Is Laurel around? *(No response.)* I just come by to...well, if she's not in I was just wonderin' if I could leave a message for her?

There is no response from JANICE. JERRY grabs a pen out of his breast pocket. He looks around for some paper. He sees the bible underneath JANICE's head and pulls it out from under her head to write a message on. When he does so her head thumps on the table and she wakes up with a start.

JANICE: Ohhhh! *(She grabs her bible from JERRY.)* W—what are you doin' here?

JERRY: I just needed to speak to Laurel if she's around. If she's not around I could leave. Or maybe come back later. It's only—

JANICE: Laurel? What do ya want to be speakin' to Laurel for?

JERRY: Just business. (*He fidgets awkwardly.*)

JANICE: Business huh? That's what I thought. Business. If that's what you're calling it nowadays. Well Laurel's not here.

                JANICE checks her watch and goes and pours a cup of tea and places it on the counter.

JERRY: (*Shifts his weight.*) And how are you doin' Janice? The weather hasn't got you down I hope. What with this rain and cold and everything?

JANICE: (*She stands as far as she can away from him in the room.*) I'm just fine.

                Awkward pause.

JERRY: And your Ma. How's she?

JANICE: Just the same.

                Pause.

JERRY: Oh, that's good. I do wish sometimes that my Ma was still with us. She was a great old woman. Stubborn but good hearted. Real sweet when she wanted to be. Well, sometimes anyway. (*Pause.*) Look, I don't suppose that you're doin' anything tonight?

JANICE: And why don't you suppose that?

JERRY: Well, what I meant was that I was hoping that you weren't because—

JANICE: Well you supposed wrong I'm afraid.

JERRY: Alright then. I apologize. I certainly—

                All of a sudden they hear the squeak of MS. QUINN's wheelchair and her voice is heard from down the hall. JANICE quiets JERRY with her hand.

MS. QUINN: Janice? Janice what's all that noise I hear?

JANICE: It's nothin' Ma. It's just Jerry. He came to speak to Laurel is all.

MS. QUINN: Laurel you say? *(Pause.)* Haddock?

JERRY: Yes ma'am.

MS. QUINN: You're here to see Laurel?

JERRY: Yes ma'am.

               Pause.

MS. QUINN: Well she's not here. *(Long pause.)* Have you gone?

JERRY: Uhhh, no ma'am.

               MS. QUINN is heard grumbling. Her wheel chair can be heard squeaking as she enters the room. JERRY and JANICE become rigid. MS. QUINN wheels in the room slowly and goes over to the counter. She grabs the teacup off the counter and then looks at JERRY suspiciously.

JERRY: *(He clears his throat.)* I was just askin' how things were over here, with the family and all. I was just wondering how the girls were managing, with you confined to your chair and not being able to work around the house.

MS. QUINN: Well, things are just fine over here.

JERRY: *(Pause.)* And you wouldn't happen to know when Laurel would be comin' home?

MS. QUINN: Why?

JERRY: Oh I just had to speak to her is—

MS. QUINN: *(Interrupts.)* About what?

JERRY: *(Nervously.)* Uhh just something about her job at the bank.

MS. QUINN: The bank is it? She was just tellin' me that she worked at the tin shop.

JERRY:	*(Quickly.)* The tin shop…is what I meant. Sure it was just a slip of the tongue. Of course I know that she works at the tin shop.
MS. QUINN:	Is that right?
JERRY:	S—Sure.

MS. QUINN wheels over to JERRY and sticks her clamper in his face.

MS. QUINN:	Do you think I'm stupid Jerry Haddock?
JERRY:	Uhh, no ma'am. No I don't.
MS. QUINN:	I know more than anyone about what goes on in this town. More than anyone.
JERRY:	Yes ma'am. Well I do know a bit, being the police officer and all. I would think that I should—
MS. QUINN:	You should what?
JERRY:	Uhhh-
MS. QUINN:	You Jerry Haddock are nothing but a joke. A monkey with a can could do a better job of protecting this town than you. Don't think you can go fooling an old woman, young man, because even though my body isn't keeping up, my mind is sharp. Sharper than ever.

She whacks him on the knee with her clamper.

And don't you forget it!

JERRY:	Ow! Al—alright. Yes ma'am.

MS. QUINN wheels herself back to her table and picks up her tea cup.

JANICE:	Laurel left this morning already. She should be back a little later.
MS. QUINN:	Shut yourself Janice.

JANICE: Yes Ma.

MS. QUINN: Will there be anything else Haddock?

JERRY: No ma'am. No there's not.

               Pause.

               W—Well then, you have yourself a fine day Ms.
               Quinn. Don't let the weather get you down now.
               They say it should be nice in a few more days.
               (Clears throat.) Goodbye.

               *She does not answer. JERRY waves his hat at
               JANICE and MS. QUINN as he leaves out the door.
               Neither respond and he is gone. JANICE looks at
               MS. QUINN to see if she is looking back at her. She
               is not and so JANICE tries to sneak out of the room.*

MS. QUINN: Janice!

JANICE: Yes Ma.

MS. QUINN: Come over here.

JANICE: Yes Ma. *(She goes over to the table.)*

MS. QUINN: *(Stares ahead.)* You don't have to throw yourself on
               every man you see. The last thing that anyone wants
               is to see you with your skirt up over your head
               making a fool out of yourself. *(Pause, looks at her.)*
               You're an ungodly thing if ever I did see one.

               JANICE does not respond.

               MS. QUINN waves her out.

               *JANICE disappears down the hall. MS. QUINN
               continues to sit at the table and she stares ahead
               frowning. She then picks up her teacup and slurps it
               very loudly. Lights down.*

Scene 3

It is night. The lights in the house are very dim. There is only a little light coming from the doorway. JERRY and LAUREL can be seen moving boxes inside. Bottles hitting each other can be heard inside the boxes. Once the boxes are safely in the corner, LAUREL turns on the lights. JERRY is not dressed in his policeman's uniform. The two of them listen carefully for any sound and JERRY checks out the window.

LAUREL: What do ya think you're checkin' for Jer? The cops?

JERRY: I don't want anyone to see us is all. I just get a little nervous. You put my horse behind the trees didn't you?

LAUREL: No one saw us, trust me.

JERRY closes the door.

LAUREL: Shhhhh! *(Whispers.)* My Ma!

JERRY: Right. Sorry.

LAUREL goes into one of the boxes and pulls out a bottle of rum. She grabs two glasses off the counter and goes over to the table to open the bottle.

LAUREL: Will you be joinin' me in a little celebration drink?

JERRY: No. *(He is still looking around nervously.)* I don't drink the stuff, I only sell it. You know that.

LAUREL: That's right noble of you. You're quite a noble guy you are. *(She laughs a little.)*

JERRY: With all the money you owe I really don't think you should be drinkin' the stuff either. You with all your debts.

LAUREL: *(Defensive.)* You shut up about my debts. They're none of your business. I can take care of myself.

JERRY: Ya well, I came by this morning to tell you that the boss won't wait much longer to get his money. *(Pause.)* Your Ma wouldn't have me here though.

LAUREL: *(She laughs a little.)* Crazy old woman.

 Pause.

JERRY: I don't suppose that Janice will be comin' home anytime soon? I was just thinking that it was a bit late and she shouldn't be out alone at this time.

LAUREL: How would I know when she'll be in? She's a grown woman, she can come home whenever she wants.

JERRY: I just thought you might know is all.

LAUREL: I don't. *(Pause.)* You wouldn't want her here anyway. She'll just cry and slobber and beg me to forgive her when she comes home. She does that every damn night it seems now.

JERRY: She wants you to forgive her?

LAUREL: She wants someone to I guess.

JERRY: *(Laughs slightly.)* I once knew a crazy old man that believed God would forgive him of his sins if he ate a page of the bible every day.

 Pause.

LAUREL: And?

JERRY: And what?

LAUREL: Was he forgiven?

JERRY: Dunno. I guess maybe he thought he was. That was good enough. Died of ink poisoning though. Shame.

LAUREL: Shame. *(Pause.)* Did he finish at least?

JERRY: Uhh. Don't know.

LAUREL: Shame if he didn't.

JERRY: Ya.

> *JERRY leans his head on the back of the chair.*
> *LAUREL stares ahead frowning.*

LAUREL: Hey Jer?

JERRY: What?

LAUREL: Would ya ever…would ya ever say that I was crazy?

JERRY: Crazy? Crazy like how?

> *He lifts his head up slightly.*

LAUREL: Like crazy, *(Whispers.)* like how my Ma is crazy.

JERRY: Your Ma?

LAUREL: Ya.

JERRY: *(He smiles slightly.)* I don't know if she's crazy.

LAUREL: That's what you think. And you're just stupid. She's obviously crazy as hell!

JERRY: She's not so crazy as you think.

LAUREL: What's that supposed to mean?

JERRY: Nothin'.

> *He straightens up.*

LAUREL: How would you know? How would you know anything about my Ma?

JERRY: I don't—I don't know anything.

LAUREL: You know somethin'. If somethin' is goin' on with my Ma you better tell me about it.

JERRY: There's nothin'. Nothin'. I swear.

LAUREL: *(She looks at him for a few moments and then she smiles slightly.)* Well that's too bad Jer. That's really too bad you can't tell me, because I was just thinkin' about somethin' that Janice told me the other day about you.

JERRY: A—about me?

LAUREL: Yes, yes about you. *(Slowly.)* Now what was it?

JERRY: What? What did she say?

LAUREL: *(Pretends to try to remember.)* See, I just can't seem to remember at all what she said. Maybe you should tell me a little somethin' first, perhaps about my Ma, just to jog my memory.

JERRY: *(Stares at her with hatred for a moment.)* Oh for Christ's sake. *(Whispers.)* I'm under strict orders never to share information.

            LAUREL stares at him. He pauses for a moment longer, sighs and then leans closer to LAUREL on the table.

            Laurel?

LAUREL: Ya.

JERRY: Laurel if you ever…

LAUREL: *(She puts her hand over her heart as if to take a vow.)* It will never leave this room.

JERRY: Alright then…I know your Ma so well because she used to work for us.

            He cringes.

LAUREL: *(She is shocked.)* No! My Ma used to run? The good Christian woman herself committing liquor crimes. Ha!

JERRY: Jesus keep your voice down! You'll wake the old thing up.

LAUREL: Right.

JERRY: She used to run here in Wadena, in the glory days of the prohibition. After your pa died she needed money.

LAUREL: Jesus Christ.

JERRY: She was damn good at it too.

LAUREL: She was good you say?

JERRY: Damn good. Made thousands in her time, maybe even more than that.

LAUREL: Thousands...

JERRY: Ya, more then she probably knew what to do with. They say she should have been the richest woman in these parts. No one knew what she did with the money though. She sure didn't live fancy or nothin'. *(Pause.)* But that's all I'm telling ya. That's all I'll say.

LAUREL: Okay Jer, alright.

            At that moment the door opens and JANICE comes into the house. She heads toward her bedroom. JERRY tries to speak to her but he only makes squeaking sounds. JANICE disappears toward her bedroom.

LAUREL: That was slick Jer.

JERRY: *(He frowns at her and then smiles.)* So what has she been sayin' about me then?

            LAUREL leans across the table as if to whisper and then smacks JERRY across the head.

            Ow! Jesus Christ. I fuckin' hate you.

            JERRY gets up and goes toward the door rubbing his head bitterly. He goes to slam the door behind him, catches himself and then shuts it softly.

            LAUREL laughs as the lights go down.

Scene 4

> *JANICE is sitting rocking in the rocking chair beside the table. She is reading her bible and she has a bottle and a glass of rum beside her. She is turning the pages slowly. She then stops, considers the bible for a moment, rips a page out of it and eats a corner of it. She is chewing it slowly when LAUREL walks into the room. She walks past JANICE without looking at her. JANICE quickly tries to hide the bottle under the table. When LAUREL has passed her she turns around and glares at JANICE in anger.*

LAUREL: That had better not be my rum you're drinkin'.

JANICE: And what if it is?

LAUREL: *(She grabs the bottle from underneath the table.)* Jesus Christ Janice. How many goddamn times have I told you?

JANICE: *(She mumbles with her mouth full of bible.)* Well maybe you shouldn't be runnin' the stuff all over the place then. It's the Devil's work Laurel.

LAUREL: You're the one who drinks it all day. I suppose drinkin' it is God's work.

> *She slams the bottle onto the counter.*

JANICE: Oh, I've got my demons Laur.

LAUREL: Don't you start with me about your demons. *(Pause.)* What the hell have you got in your mouth?

JANICE: Nothin'. *(She swallows.)*

> *Pause.*

You know, if dad were alive he'd put an end to your runnin' right away.

LAUREL: Ya well, I guess that won't be happening, since you murdered the poor bastard!

JANICE: Laurel! Do ya have to always talk about it? You just can't let things lie can you?

LAUREL: *(She tidies up the counter.)* There are some things I can't. It's the truth ain't it?

JANICE: It was just an accident, I was only a young thing.

               She hugs her bible to her chest.

LAUREL: I was there Janice, you don't have to tell me. I know what a rotten old drunk he was. He deserved it.

JANICE: I wish you wouldn't talk about it anymore, you and Ma.

LAUREL: All I care about is you keeping your nose out of my life. I got better things to worry about than you drinkin' all of my bottles. And you know what Ma will do if she catches you.

JANICE: What does she say about me Laurel?

LAUREL: What do you mean?

JANICE: She said something about me didn't she?

LAUREL: She didn't say nothin' about you.

JANICE: Bad stuff? Has she been sayin' any bad stuff about me?

LAUREL: What? Like you're a stupid old drunk?

JANICE: Is that what she said about me?

LAUREL: No, that's what I say about you.

JANICE: *(Frightened.)* She really hates me, she really does.

LAUREL: It's just our Ma. She's a crazy old woman.

JANICE: And you know what else? She's always watchin' us, always listenin'. Did you know that sometimes she'll even listen at the doors with a glass?

JANICE demonstrates with her own glass.

LAUREL: She does no such thing. That's just stupid.

             Pause.

JANICE: Laurel?

LAUREL: What.

JANICE: Do ya think maybe she wants to…get rid of me?

LAUREL: Who?

JANICE: Our Ma. *(Whispers.)* I think our Ma wants to…murder me or something.

LAUREL: *(Pauses for a moment.)* What the hell is wrong with you?

JANICE: She's wanted to for years, I just know it. Ever since I done away with our pa. *(JANICE gets up from the chair.)*

LAUREL: Shut up, I don't want to hear this shit.

JANICE: She'll get me when I'm sleeping, or maybe she'll poison me or something. Something slow and painful. God save me. I can't hardly bare it any longer. I can't!

LAUREL: You don't know what you're talking about Janice, just shut your face.

JANICE: You wouldn't care anyway. Both of you never forgave me. My whole life.

LAUREL: You're being an idiot. A drunken idiot.

JANICE: You're just like our Ma, Laurel. Just like her. You even talk like her.

LAUREL: *(Glaring.)* You take that back, you take it back right now. *(She walks toward JANICE slowly.)*

JANICE: I won't. I won't because it's the truth. *(Cowering slightly.)*

            LAUREL turns on her. JANICE grabs what she thinks is her bible off the kitchen counter and holds it in front of her for protection against LAUREL.

            God is the only one that forgives me Laurel. Not you, not Ma, only God.

            LAUREL looks at her and then knocks the book out of her hand.

LAUREL: That's my fuckin' cookbook Janice.

            JANICE turns around and begins to frantically search for her bible.

JANICE: You're even crazy like her. You're crazy like our Ma.

LAUREL: That's it!

            LAUREL suddenly grabs the real bible from the table and runs across the room. She holds the pages as if she's about to rip them out.

            Take it back Janice!

JANICE: Give it! Give it back, it's all I've got. *(She jumps toward LAUREL)*

LAUREL: *(Jumps out of JANICE's way.)* Take it back. Take back what you said!

JANICE: Don't Laurel! It's my only one.

LAUREL: If God really loved you he wouldn't have made you fat. Did you ever think of that? Huh Janice?

JANICE: *(Growls in frustration at LAUREL.)* Grrrrr—

LAUREL: You're the one who's just like our Ma. You're fat like her and you're crazy like her!

            JANICE lunges for her bible and LAUREL jumps out of her way. JANICE chases LAUREL around the kitchen. LAUREL trips and JANICE tackles her to the ground where they wrestle over the bible. JANICE sits on LAUREL's stomach and tries to pry the bible from her hands. The bible finally flies across the floor and MS. QUINN stops it with her foot just as she is coming out of her bedroom. LAUREL and JANICE remain on the floor. MS. QUINN bends down in her chair and picks it up. She wheels her squeaky chair over to the stove and drops the bible into the top of it. During this time JANICE and LAUREL remain tangled on the floor. MS. QUINN then wheels herself slowly out of the room. Lights down as the wheels of the chair continue to squeak.

Scene 5

Lights come up dimly on MS. QUINN who is sleeping in her bed. The lamp near her bed is on. We hear the living room clock strike 11. The door to her bedroom opens slowly and JANICE comes into the room with the poker from the fireplace in her hand. She shuts the door to the bedroom. She crosses over to the opposite side of the bed from the door and stands over her mother for a moment.

JANICE: *(Whispering.)* Ma?...Ma?

There is no response from MS. QUINN. JANICE grips the poker in both hands and stares at it for a long time. She finally makes up her mind, closes her eyes and stands back. At that moment the doorknob to the room turns. JANICE hits the floor. The door slowly opens and LAUREL comes into the room. She is carrying the meat knife from the kitchen. JANICE is peering under the bed and she realizes who has come into the room.

(Stands up quickly, whispers.) Laurel?!

LAUREL is startled and cries out. She then drops the knife onto the floor.

LAUREL: Fuck!!

             *For fear of waking their mother up, the two sisters hit
             the floor simultaneously. The girls are motionless.
             After a few moments the two of them lift their heads
             over the edge of the bed at the same time and peer over
             at their mother. She is still. The two stand up slowly
             and stare at each other wide-eyed. They talk in loud
             whispers for the rest of the scene.*

JANICE: What the hell are you doing?

LAUREL: What the hell am *I* doing? What the hell are *you*
             doing?

JANICE: I'm…checkin' on mom is all.

LAUREL: Checkin' on mom.

JANICE: Ya.

LAUREL: With a poker.

JANICE: I was tendin' the fire and I come to check on Ma.

LAUREL: Bull.

JANICE: And you. I suppose you was cookin' a meal and you
             just thought you'd come in here and see how she
             was?

LAUREL: No. I come in here to kill 'er. Just like you.

JANICE: Well, Jesus Christ.

LAUREL: *(Amused.)* Look at you, using the Lord's name in
             vain.

JANICE: So what the hell are we going to do now?

             Pause.

LAUREL: Just what we came here to do.

JANICE: This is crazy!

LAUREL: We're crazy, God knows we come by it honestly.

               Pause.

JANICE: So who's it gonna be?

LAUREL: Huh?

JANICE: Who's gonna, ya know—

               She makes stabbing motions with her hand.

LAUREL: Oh. I guess you should.

JANICE: Me?! And why is that?

LAUREL: Because you're better at these types of things.

JANICE: Laurel!

LAUREL: Plus, a poker is a lot cleaner. I wouldn't know where
               to stab her.

JANICE: Jesus. It's not that hard.

LAUREL: Fine! Give me the damn poker.

               *JANICE hands her the poker and LAUREL feels its
               weight in her hands.*

               Alright?

JANICE: Alright.

               *LAUREL wields the poker over her head with two
               hands.*

               Wait!

LAUREL: What?!

JANICE: It doesn't feel right.

LAUREL: What? It's not like the last time you killed one of our
               parents?

JANICE: I mean like we should at least pray for her or something.

LAUREL: Pray?

JANICE: Ya, I never prayed for dad.

LAUREL: Oh boy.

JANICE: I would really feel a lot better if we prayed Laur. She's our Ma.

LAUREL: Will ya shut up afterwards?

JANICE: Ya.

LAUREL: Hurry up then.

              JANICE kneels beside her mother's bed. She prepares to pray and closes her eyes. Before she begins she glances up at her sister and gestures to suggest that she should kneel too. After rolling her eyes LAUREL finally kneels on the other side of the bed. She places the poker beside her mother on the bed.

JANICE: *(She prays.)* Hello Father. It's Janice and Laurel here. You'll be findin' us today in a rather bizarre little situation but since you are such a loving Father I know that you'll at least listen to what I has to say.

              LAUREL clears her throat.

              I was just wonderin' Father if you would take pity on the soul of our mother—

LAUREL: Even though she's a selfish old bitch.

JANICE: *(Over LAUREL's voice.)* We're prayin' for the soul of our mother and if you could take pity on her we'd be real grateful. Amen. *(She begins to stand up.)*

LAUREL: Wait.

JANICE: What?

LAUREL: What about us?

JANICE: What *about* us?

LAUREL: We got souls too.

JANICE: Ya so?

LAUREL: So pray for our souls.

JANICE: It doesn't work that way.

LAUREL: C'mon Jan. What hurt could it do really?

JANICE: *(She kneels back down.)* This is a little awkward now Father but Laurel was just thinkin' that I should mention that we had souls too. I guess what I'm askin' is that if you're feelin' real gracious today, you could maybe have a little mercy for our souls. Like, just a little. We're not asking for a whole l—

LAUREL: Okay, that'll do.

JANICE: You can't rush prayer.

LAUREL: I think that these are very special circumstances.

JANICE: Fine. *(Stands up.)* Even if He might have been considering saving our souls, He won't now. He's up there right now sayin' "Oh, I was about to save the souls of those nice girls down there but they can't even be bother—

LAUREL: You said you'd shut up Jan!

JANICE: I'm shut.

        Pause.

LAUREL: Will you count to three for me then, and then I'll… *(Waves the poker in the air.)*

JANICE: Ya okay. *(She shuts her eyes.)* One… Two… Three!

        LAUREL still does not bring the poker down on their mother.

Three!

Pause.

Laurel, Three!

LAUREL: I know three!

JANICE: So…

LAUREL: So…I can't do it.

JANICE: Oh…

LAUREL: I can't do it. *(Pause.)* I'm just a horrible person is what I am. *(She sits down on a chair near her mother's bed.)*

JANICE: I'm a horrible person too, I couldn't have done it either. *(She comes and crouches beside LAUREL.)*

The two sisters sit and stare at their mother for a while. They are both still holding their weapons.

LAUREL: Old fuck.

Pause.

JANICE: We'd better be off to bed Laurel, before the old thing wakes up.

LAUREL: I suppose.

They both stand up.

(Sigh.) G'night Janice.

JANICE: G'night Laurel.

They turn off the lamp in the room and the stage goes black.

MS. QUINN: G'night girls.

Scene 6

> *The lights come up dimly on the space just outside the front door. The audience cannot see the inside of the house but a light above the door outside is on. It is night. JERRY and LAUREL can be heard groaning as they carry something heavy. LAUREL carries a lantern on top of her box. They then emerge into the light, both carrying boxes filled with bottles. When they reach the door they set the boxes down and breathe heavily. JERRY sits on his box and wipes his forehead with a handkerchief.*

JERRY: Jesus Laurel, that's quite the load.

LAUREL: It's my biggest one yet.

JERRY: How the hell are you going to get rid of all of that? Last time I got a load that big, it was more trouble than it was worth to get rid of it. Why I—

LAUREL: I got debts to pay off so I'll find a way alright?

> *She gets up.*

JERRY: Hang on a sec, let me rest a minute.

LAUREL: Ya rested four times on our way from the wagon.

JERRY: I told you I have a bad back. It's the weather. It gets right down into my back and the bones—

LAUREL: You do not have a bad back.

JERRY: Do too. It's been bad for years.

LAUREL: You're just fat is what you are.

JERRY: *(Offended.)* I'm not that fat. What a thing to say. Fat.

LAUREL: *(Under her breath.)* Fat enough.

JERRY: Well you're a delight.

LAUREL: *(She prods him.)* Can we go now? I already promised I'd help you with your boxes in the morning.

Pause.

JERRY: My boxes?

LAUREL: Ya, your boxes. Your rum Jerry. *(She gets up.)* For you to sell.

                Pause.

JERRY: What if I don't want my boxes in the morning? Huh? W—What if I never want to get anymore boxes again?

LAUREL: *(She sits back down on her box.)* Not this shit again. Is this about the fat comment 'cause I'm sorry.

JERRY: How many years have I been doing this now? How many years have I been breaking the law that I'm supposed to enforce?

LAUREL: *(Annoyed.)* Ever since you were small enough to fit through the underground tunnels Jer. You've told me many times.

JERRY: And I said that when I started in on the police force, I would quit all this.

LAUREL: *(Bored.)* Mmmm. And ya never—

JERRY: And I never did. And 15 years later, I'm still here, with these damn boxes, hopin' someone won't see us.

LAUREL: Trust me Jer. You can get away with murder in a small town like this. I wouldn't worry.

JERRY: I can't go on doin' this Laurel. It grates on me everyday. I need to settle down. It's about time for me.

LAUREL: Oh Jesus.

JERRY: I'm serious Laurel, this town depends on me and I've got people to protect.

LAUREL: Alright Jer.

JERRY: *(Ignores her.)* I think I might get married, take up boating in my free time. Maybe have some kids or something. It's what I've always really wanted.

LAUREL: Take up boating? In the prairies?

JERRY: Well, maybe not boating, maybe gardening.

LAUREL: Gardening.

JERRY: Ya gardening. Anything but this.

LAUREL: You're good at this.

JERRY: I could be good at other things.

LAUREL: Like gardening.

JERRY: Like gardening.

LAUREL: I really don't care what you do Jer, just help me get these boxes into the house.

JERRY: You don't believe me do you? Tomorrow, when we pick up our load, I'll tell the boss that I'm done. That this is the last time. I'll tell him that I'm retiring from the business and that there's nothing he can do to stop me. *(He gets up from his box and goes to lift it.)*

LAUREL: Okay Jer.

               She picks up her own box.

JERRY: You'll see Laurel. I'm a good guy from now on. A good guy and a great officer.

               He gives the door a hard kick to open it but something is blocking the way and the door comes back.

LAUREL: What the hell? *(She also goes to the door and kicks it even harder, a thud is heard.)*

               The two of them set down their boxes and look at each other. They shove the door open as far as it will go and then step inside. LAUREL turns on the light and MS. QUINN in lying on the floor next to her wheelchair. There is a glass in her hand.

LAUREL: Ma?

                    Pause.

JERRY: Ms. Quinn?

                    Pause, they look at each other.

JERRY: Jesus Laurel. We kicked her head right in.

LAUREL: We? No, not *we* Jer. You. *You're* the one what gave the first kick, not me.

                    LAUREL kneels down and puts her head over her mother's heart. After a moment she stands up.

LAUREL: Fuck.

                    Lights down.

Scene 7

                    Lights come up on LAUREL who is standing beside her mother's rocking chair. She has propped up her mother in the chair and is staring at her body in concern. She crosses MS. QUINN's arms one way and then the other until she is satisfied with her appearance. She then stands beside her mother with her own arms crossed. Footsteps are heard from the hallway. JANICE appears in her housecoat and slippers holding another bible. She walks into the room and when she sees her mother she becomes nervous.

JANICE: Morning Laurel! Morning Ma!

                    She goes over to the counter and pours herself some coffee. She then goes and stands beside LAUREL.

                    (She whispers to LAUREL.) Sleepin' in her chair eh?

LAUREL does not respond and stares blankly ahead.

Has she said anything about the other night to you yet?

LAUREL does not respond.

Ya, me neither. *(She looks over at her mother nervously.)* Frankly I think we should talk to her about it.

Pause.

She might forgive us for what we tried to do. Ya never know. We could just ask.

No response.

(Sigh.) I don't know about you, but I can't live with this over my head.

LAUREL looks at her. JANICE then moves toward her mother and stands over her.

(She takes a deep breath.) ...Ma?

Pause.

Ma? *(JANICE is confused.)* Ma, Laurel and I, we just wanted to...

JANICE tries to shake her mother slightly and when she does so her mother falls to the floor in a heap. JANICE stares at her mother for a moment, looks up at LAUREL, and then points at their mother. LAUREL avoids JANICE's gaze.

Oh God. What's happened?

JANICE leans over her mother and listens for her heart.

(Whispers.) Laurel? I think she's dead.

LAUREL nods.

Oh God. *(She moves slowly toward the table.)* Oh God.

She drops her bible on the table.

I don't know what happened. I can't even begin to think.

She is frantic and sits down.

LAUREL: *(Sigh.)* She's been dead for a while Janice.

JANICE: When? Did she die yesterday? This morning? When?

LAUREL: Last night.

JANICE: I—I can't even begin to think. Oh God was it something I did? Was it something I did?

LAUREL: Just settle down there—

JANICE: Oh God. What if it was something I did. Oh God, I don't remember.

Pause. LAUREL thinks hard for a moment.

LAUREL: *(Slowly.)* Janice?

JANICE: What?

LAUREL: You did remember to give Ma her pills yesterday, didn't you?

JANICE: Her pills?

LAUREL: Yes Janice, her pills. You did remember them.

JANICE: I— Oh God. Oh God I don't remember. *(She clutches her bible to her chest.)*

LAUREL: You know that Ma has to take her pills every day.

JANICE: I know that. I know she does.

LAUREL: You didn't remember, did you Janice? You were drinkin' yesterday and you forgot.

JANICE: Maybe I was. I don't remember. I don't remember yesterday.

LAUREL: Oh no. Oh no.

JANICE: Oh don't Laurel. *(She covers her ears.)* Don't.

LAUREL: What have you done?

JANICE: I didn't mean to Laurel. It was an accident.

LAUREL: But you knew she had to take her pills. You knew.

JANICE: I—I don't remember. I don't remember anything.

LAUREL: You didn't remember anything about Dad either Janice.

            Pause.

            Did you?

JANICE: *(Quietly.)* What are we going to do?

LAUREL: *(She stares ahead.)* I don't know Janice.

JANICE: Could you ever forgive me for this?

LAUREL: Don't know.

JANICE: Are you going to turn me in Laurel? Are you gonna say it was all me?

LAUREL: *(She thinks for a moment.)* I guess the best thing we could do for you would be to say she had a heart attack.

JANICE: Oh! Would you say that? Would you say that for me?

            Pause.

LAUREL: I guess that's what we'll say.

JANICE: Oh thank you. Thank you! *(She gets up out of her chair.)*

LAUREL: You have to promise me something though Janice.

JANICE: Anything.

LAUREL: You have to promise me that this will be our secret. This arrangement. You can't tell anyone.

JANICE: I promise Laurel. *(She places her hand on her bible.)* I swear.

LAUREL: Good...good.

JANICE goes to hug LAUREL but she pushes her away in disgust. JANICE does not take particular offense to this.

JANICE: I'd best be getting dressed then.

She walks out of the room and steps over her mother's body as she leaves.

LAUREL: Help me get her back in the chair at least.

JANICE: Oh.

She and LAUREL bend down to lift their mother. They struggle for some time under the weight of her body. They try several times and finally lift her into her chair. LAUREL folds her arms again in the same position. JANICE fixes her mother's hair tenderly. Satisfied with their work, they stand back. After a few moments, MS. QUINN once again slides to the floor. Lights down.

Scene 8

It is afternoon and raining. JANICE, LAUREL and JERRY enter. They are returning from the bank. LAUREL is smiling and carrying a safety deposit box. JANICE is weepy and she clutches her bible to her chest. JANICE pours herself a drink, sits down at the table and stares blankly ahead. LAUREL goes to the cupboard to get a knife and JERRY stands awkwardly in the corner. He is disheveled and looks like he hasn't slept in days. He has brought some brownies on a plate. They all remain there for a moment without saying anything. Throughout the beginning of the scene LAUREL tries to pry the lid off the deposit box with a large grin on her face.

JERRY: *(He places the brownies on the table in front of JANICE.)* I brought you some brownies there. *(Pause.)* I baked them myself.

JANICE: That was right nice of you Jerry.

              She continues to stare ahead blankly and sniffles.

              JERRY motions as if he is going to put his arm around her and then he recoils. He does this again and then backs away. JANICE does not see him do this.

JERRY: A—And the funeral is what time?

JANICE: *(Still rather dazed.)* Huh? Oh, 3 o'clock.

              Pause.

JERRY: *(Hopefully.)* I—I was just wondering if you had a date. I mean…someone to go with to the funeral.

JANICE: Yes Jerry, Laurel and me will go over together.

              LAUREL gives up on the box just for a moment and comes to take a brownie off the table.

LAUREL: *(Hurriedly.)* That's right, Janice and me are goin' over in just a little while. I guess we'll see you there then?

JERRY: *(Pause.)* Right, right I best be goin'. Best be gettin' ready for the funeral.

LAUREL: Yep. You could come back later and give us a ride though.

JERRY: Oh! Oh sure, yes.

             JERRY turns to leave and then looks back at JANICE. He begins to open his mouth to speak when LAUREL shoots him a look. He stops and then heads out the door. He shuts the door behind him and LAUREL picks up JANICE's drink and raises it to the closed door before downing it. She then throws the rest of her brownie on the table.

LAUREL: That's the most disgusting piece of shit I've ever tasted.

JANICE: Thanks again Laurel.

LAUREL: Huh? *(She is busy with the box.)* Oh ya sure. No problem.

JANICE: Now I'm serious. Not many people would do that for their sister.

LAUREL: Don't mention it.

JANICE: I mean, no one else in the world would have ever forgiven me for that. I—

LAUREL: *(Ignoring what JANICE is saying.)* What's in this box is gonna get rid of all of our problems. This must have been where mom kept all her runnin' money. Savin' it for a rainy day she was. Well it's rainin' now!

JANICE: I don't know if it will get rid of *all* of our problems. *(She raises her glass in front of her face.)*

             The lid on the safety deposit box finally comes loose.

LAUREL: Ah ha! Janice, help me get this off.

             No response.

             Janice! Get your big old ass over here and help me with this.

             JANICE gets up reluctantly to help her. The two

struggle with the box and finally get the lid off. When they do they stare inside, their expressions blank. They both look at each other. LAUREL then slowly picks up the box and holds it upside down. Two dolls fall out of the box suspended by nooses around their necks. One doll is holding a bible and a bottle of rum, the other doll is holding a knife. The two stare at each other for a long time. Finally LAUREL puts the box right side up and places the two dolls carefully inside. She stares ahead blankly.

JANICE: Oh God Laur, oh God. *(She reaches inside the box, picks up the doll with her likeness and strokes it.)*

                   Pause.

                   It's because He knows. God knows what I did. He knows—

LAUREL: Shut up Janice.

JANICE: *(Almost in tears.)* He knows what I did and so he's sent this to us. He doesn't care—

LAUREL: Shut up! I told you to shut up! *(She knocks the box out of JANICE's hand and stomps on it.)* I don't want to hear your voice. I don't want to hear your voice talking to me about God. He has never even given us the time of day Jan, never!

JANICE: Oh no, oh no, don't be sayin' those things, don't be. *(She opens up her bible on the table.)* Here. Oh here. "To open their eyes and turn them from darkness to light, and from the power of Satan to God, so that they may receive forgiveness of sins and a place among those who are sanctified by faith—"

                   LAUREL grabs the knife that she used to open the safety deposit box and stabs it through the middle of the bible. JANICE gasps. LAUREL stares at her for a few more seconds and then goes over to the counter and pours herself a drink.

JANICE: *(She stares in shock at her bible for a few moments and then bursts into tears.)* Why did ya do that Laur? I killed our pa and I killed our Ma and now I got a knife through my bible.

           She continues crying and LAUREL stares at her with hatred for a moment.

LAUREL: Shut up, stop cryin'.

JANICE: Oh, what am I gunna do? I haven't got a hope anymore.

LAUREL: Oh! And I suppose you're the one that deserves all the pity, all the sympathy. *(Sarcastically.)* Well poor you. Drinkin' all the time, chasin' away your demons. Poor Jan, she's got an excuse for bein' a failure. She's got something to cry about.

JANICE: *(Sniffs.)* I got more to cry about than you. *(She continues crying.)*

LAUREL: Stop it. Stop cryin'!

JANICE: I'm doomed Laur, I'm doomed for sure.

LAUREL: You're not doomed Jan.

JANICE: Don't even say that I'm not. I don't got a chance.

LAUREL: *(She is fed up and hysterical.)* You're not doomed because you never killed our pa! I killed him!

           JANICE stops crying and slowly looks up at LAUREL.

JANICE: What? *(Pause.)* That's a lie. That's a dirty lie. I know I did it, Ma told me. She told me so many times that I was the one that pushed him in front of the train. She made me pay—

LAUREL: She said it was you because you were too young to get in trouble with the law. She said it so I wouldn't have to go to jail. You were only seven years old

Janice. God, you're so stupid. You always were so fat, stupid, and fat.

JANICE is breathing hard and staring at LAUREL.

JANICE: You're a liar. You're a damn liar and I don't believe you for a second. Ma would never have done that for you.

LAUREL: Well she did.

JANICE: She didn't.

LAUREL: She did Janice. She did. And now you can stop your crying for God's sake.

JANICE: I'm the one that killed him Laurel. I remember all of it.

LAUREL: You remember nothing. You told me so many times you remembered nothing.

JANICE: You—You're a liar.

LAUREL: *(Sarcastically.)* Oh, so now you're demons have flown away on you then. There's no more demons to keep you company? Poor poor Janny. All alone.

JANICE: Shut up Laurel, shut up!

JANICE grabs the knife out of her bible and wields it at LAUREL.

You're a liar!

LAUREL: A liar am I?

LAUREL grabs the poker from beside the fireplace. JANICE and LAUREL circle around each other.

I think I should know. I saw his face while he was fallin'. I saw the way he tried to grab for the both of us when he fell. Like he was tryin' to put us in front of the train instead of himself.

JANICE: He never did, he never did that at all.

LAUREL: Oh yes he did. He did just that. He was an old drunk what didn't even love us. Only cared about himself.

JANICE: You know who you're talkin' like Laurel? You're talkin' just like our Ma used to talk. You're just as crazy as her.

LAUREL: Me?! You think *I'm* the one that's like Ma? Who's the one that's fat like her? Who's the one that drinks like a fish just like Ma used to? Huh? Talking about God in her drunken states.

JANICE: I hate you Laurel! I hate you!

> *At that moment JERRY bursts in through the door and it hits the back wall. He runs over to JANICE, picks her up and kisses her.*

> *The three are speechless for a few moments. After this, LAUREL's face turns from confusion to annoyance.*

LAUREL: Jerry, what the hell are you doing?

JERRY: I—I'm not going to hold it back anymore. No more games. I've come to tell Janice—

LAUREL: It's not a good time right now. You'd better just leave.

JERRY: I—I won't leave unless Janice asks me to herself.

JANICE: What's that you come to tell me Jerry?

LAUREL: He's just saying nonsense, pay no attention to him.

JANICE: I didn't ask you.

JERRY: I—I just come to give you my confession of love, once and for all. Just so I know one way or the other if we can…be together.

JANICE: Oh, well that's quite the confession.

LAUREL: Jesus Christ! You're just making a fool of yourself Jerry.

JANICE: Is he now?

LAUREL: Just go home already. There is something going on between Janice and me that we're not finished discussing. *(She raises her poker again.)*

JANICE: *(Glares at LAUREL.)* I think you should stay. Come and sit down awhile.

> *JANICE forces JERRY into a chair. JANICE is on one side and LAUREL is on the other. They both still have their weapons in hand.*

What was that you were just saying? You were saying that you loved me weren't you?

JERRY: I was yes.

LAUREL: You mean that you think you love her. But do you even really know her Jer?

JERRY: Well I think I—

JANICE: And if you loved me, would you take me away from this place with you? Take me away from this house? Would you take me away from Laurel?

JERRY: That—

LAUREL: Tell me something, both of you. *(Slowly.)* Would you be able to live with someone and love them if they had a horrible secret? If you found out something they had done and it was something awful?

> *Both JANICE and JERRY become rigid.*

JANICE: B—But you could just take them away from their past so they could forget about it.

JERRY: I agree. I—

LAUREL: Let's say you found out from a certain somebody that this person had done something so awful that God himself didn't even love them anymore. Would you still want them to leave with you?

JERRY: Well I— I—

JANICE: But then what if it were a mistake? You would be able to forgive the person then.

JERRY: Ya!

LAUREL: But what if you couldn't prove that.

JERRY: Oh God!

JANICE: You—You can't bear this can you? You can't bear the fact that I could leave right now, without you, and you'd be left here all alone.

LAUREL: Ha! That's a laugh that is.

JANICE: Tell her. Tell her that we're leaving right now and that I'll never have to come back.

JERRY: I—

LAUREL: Oh but wait. We haven't all shared our secrets yet with each other. We haven't had our little story time yet.

JANICE: No! Set her straight Jerry! Go on. You're the police officer.

LAUREL: Ha! Don't make me laugh!

JERRY: Ahhhh! *(He screams and puts his hands over his ears.)* I'm sorry. I'm sorry for everything. I have to leave. I have to get out of here. I can't deal with this. Where's my hat? Where is it?

            Stands up and knocks the poker out of LAUREL's hand.

            Ahhh!

            Goes toward the door and trips over the landing.

            I can't! *(He leaves.)*

                Long pause, the two stare after him.

JANICE: What the hell is wrong with him?

LAUREL: Don't know. It's like he's crazy or something.

JANICE: Jesus. He could be dangerous. Going off the hinge like that.

LAUREL: Sure could. Damn violent.

> *They stare after him for a few more moments and then LAUREL picks up her poker again and considers it. The two of them look repeatedly from their weapons to each other. At the same time they slowly raise their weapons to each other's throats again.*

JANICE: Okay look Laurel. Look. We'll make a deal here. *(Pause.)* I'll forgive you for killing our pa if you forgive me for killing our Ma.

> *Pause.*

LAUREL: Okay, deal.

> *They both lower their weapons. Footsteps are then heard outside the door. JERRY opens the door, he is more calm than when he left. He tries to hide the fact that he is still frazzled.*

JERRY: I was just thinking… I just came to say… Well… It's about three now if the two of you still…you know…wanted a ride in my wagon.

LAUREL: Is it three?

> *All three look at their watches.*

JANICE: Yes.

LAUREL: Yes.

JERRY: Yes.

> *JANICE and LAUREL place their weapons on the table. LAUREL brushes off JANICE's bible and hands it to her.*

LAUREL: Good brownies by the way.

JERRY: Thanks. I made them myself.

They exit. Lights down.

The End.

Shades of Brown

Primrose Madayag Knazan

Shades of Brown was first produced at the Winnipeg Fringe Festival 2002 by i_rose_productions. It was subsequently produced in August, 2002, as part of the Fringe Festival holdovers at the Gas Station Theatre.

Written with generous support from the Manitoba Arts Council and the Winnipeg Arts Advisory Council.

Description

White, red, yellow, black, we're all just shades of brown.

Characters

SIENNA: *The Coconut,* brown on the outside, white on the inside.
Sienna is Asian and has a fuller body type.

MALAYA: *The FOB,* fresh off the boat.
Malaya is Asian, with a slight Filipino accent, but heavier as a child.

SANDY: *The Rice Lover,* a white girl with mostly Asian friends. She is blond.

Set and Costumes

Set is minimal, using boxes or chairs for different scenes. Tinikling Poles (thick bamboo poles, approx 8ft. long, wrapped in colourful tape) are used for two dance scenes. When playing main characters (Sienna, Malaya, Sandy), actors are natural. When playing other characters (teacher, mother, kids, etc.) actors wear brown or white masks, regardless of skin colour of actor.

The Coconut, The Fob and the Rice Lover

Philippine national anthem plays.

Lights up, girls hold half-brown/half-white masks.

SIENNA: Coconut.

MALAYA: Fob.

SANDY: Rice Lover.

SIENNA: Brown on the outside, white on the inside.

MALAYA: Fresh off the boat.

SANDY: Just love those Asian boys.

SIENNA: Oreo Cookie.

MALAYA: Eggroll.

SANDY: Kraft Dinner.

SIENNA: Banana.

MALAYA: Imported goods.

SANDY: Pale ale.

SIENNA: Converted rice.

MALAYA: Fried rice.

SANDY: White rice.

SIENNA: Flip.

MALAYA: Immigrant.

SANDY: Bimbo.

SIENNA: Caucasian groupie.

MALAYA: Island girl.

SANDY: Asiaphile.

SIENNA: Wannabe White.

MALAYA: Wannabe Canadian.

SANDY: Wannabe Asian.

SIENNA: White-wash.

MALAYA: Chink.

SANDY: Honky.

SIENNA: You'll never belong.

MALAYA: You'll never be one of us.

SANDY: You'll never fit in.

SIENNA: You forgot where you came from.

MALAYA: Go back to where you came from.

SANDY: You don't even know where you came from.

SIENNA: *You* don't belong here!

MALAYA: You *don't* belong here!

SANDY: You don't belong *here!*

> *Fade down to center spotlight, girls pass through spotlight as they say their lines, putting on different masks as they pass through light.*

SIENNA: Sometimes, I don't think I belong anywhere.

MALAYA: I would do anything to fit in.

SANDY: I'm always performing.

SIENNA: I do my dance.

MALAYA: I say my lines.

SANDY: I sing my song.

ALL: I wear my mask. Maybe I'll fit in now.

           Fade out.

           Kain Na! *(Eat Now.)*

           Lights fade up.

SANDY: Lumpia Shanghai with chili sweet and sour sauce. Throw in some pancit and I'm a happy camper.

SIENNA: Pergoies with koulbassa. I prefer them fried rather than boiled. Mix the sour cream with ketchup and voila—the perfect meal.

MALAYA: My favourite food is Dim Sum, but I'm bad at chopsticks. Sometimes I have to use a fork.

SANDY: I could do without cheeseburgers and fish-n-chips.

SIENNA: I don't need to eat rice everyday.

MALAYA: I'm not born with the ability to use sticks as utensils.

           Centre spotlight on SANDY.

SANDY: I am white, but not so white. My friends call me an 'Honourary Asian'. I grew up with Filipino friends. I've dated a few, or a lot, of Asian guys. Someone once called me 'Siopao'—It's this steamed Filipino rice bun filled with barbecued pork in a sweet brown sauce—Oh, forget about it. You'd get it if you were Filipino... or someone like me who's the next best thing. My Filipino "Fetish"—as some people like to call it—started many years ago with the food. Doesn't it always start with the food?

           Lights up. A young FILIPINO GIRL wearing a brown mask pulls SANDY into her house.

FILIPINO
GIRL: I come to your house all the time and your mom is always making fish sticks and dollar chips. It's my

	mom's turn to feed you. Don't worry, you'll like it. Everybody likes pancit.

SANDY: Is there fish in it? I don't like fish.

FILIPINO
GIRL: No fish—well, there's these fish ball things, but you won't even know they're there. It's mostly noodles.

SANDY: Like spaghetti?

FILIPINO
GIRL: Not really. Kind of like Chow Mein.

SANDY: I like Chow Mein.

FILIPINO
GIRL: Then you'll love pancit.

LOLA: *(With thick Filipino accent from offstage.)* Nic Nic, you ask your friend if she wants to eat.

FILIPINO
GIRL: Okay, Lola. Come on, while there's still lots.

               Pulling SANDY into another room.

SANDY: Oh my God, there's so much. Do you eat this much all the time?

FILIPINO
GIRL: It's my Nanay's birthday today and most of my relatives already came over, but some more are coming later.

SANDY: I was amazed. I was introduced to this exotic new cuisine by my next door neighbour. It was like Folklorama right at my doorstep. There was pancit—

FILIPINO
GIRL: Rice noodles with slivers of marinated vegetables, pork and chicken.

SANDY: And lumpia—

FILIPINO
GIRL: Miniature eggrolls of ground pork fried in a rice wrapping.

SANDY: And puto—

FILIPINO
GIRL: White cupcakes made of rice flour.

SANDY: And suman—

FILIPINO
GIRL: Sweet sticky rice steamed in banana leaves.

SANDY: There were a lot of rice products.

FILIPINO
GIRL: Do you like it?

SANDY: *(With mouth full.)* Oh my God, this is all so good! I'm gonna come here all the time!

>   *Spotlight.*

I was there all the time, up until Nicole moved to Lindenwoods and I went off to high school. But by then, the seed had already been planted and I was well on my way to becoming a brown girl that only looks white on the outside—like siopao, white on the outside, brown like stew on the inside.

>   *Fade out.*

Akoy Filipino

>   *Centre spotlight.*

SIENNA: *(Starts singing the first few words of "Akoy Filipino" very loudly and slightly off key.) Akoy Pilipino… Akoy Pilipino… Akoy Pilipino…*

That's all I know. I don't remember where I had first heard the song. Maybe it was at the Filipino Pavillion—don't ask me which one, I can't tell the difference. Probably on the radio, the Filipino station—I don't listen to it. My mom does, in the mornings.

Akoy Filipino...I am Filipino. That's one of the few phrases I know. Although it doesn't really apply to me. Don't get me wrong. I am a Filipino. My skin is brown. But inside, I'm as white as snow. Yes, I admit it. I am whitewash, whiteout, wannabe white girl, a coconut, banana, Twinkie, Oreo cookie, a Hostess cupcake, a Cadbury Easter Egg, and every other food that has a white filling. It's not that I always wanted to be this way...okay, maybe a part of me did. But I couldn't help it.

I am a product of my environment. I grew up in front of the boob tube watching *Gem and the Holograms* and *Full House* and eventually moved on to more mature programming such as *Baywatch* and *Beverly Hills 90210*. Try this as an experiment. Strap a brown baby to a chair in front of a Brady Bunch marathon and after a few years let's see what colour she thinks her skin is. Look around you at the next big sale at the Gap and I think you'll have your answer.

I was once a full-fledged Filipino brown girl, but *they* made me into something different, and once this happened, there was no turning back.

> *Lights up, TEACHER wearing white mask calls over SIENNA and her MOTHER who wears brown mask. MOTHER has thick Filipino accent.*

TEACHER: Mrs. Cruz, thank you for coming. I'm Sienna's kindergarten teacher.

MOTHER: What is this about? Is Sienna in trouble? Does she talk too much?

TEACHER: No, not at all. In fact, the complete opposite. Sienna is very quiet in class, especially during group discussions and games. She keeps to herself and doesn't play with the other children.

MOTHER: Sienna is very talkative when she's home. Sometimes, she talks too much. And she is laughing all the time.

TEACHER: Unfortunately, we don't see that side of her in class. There have been many times when I have tried to get Sienna to participate more, but she often gives me a blank stare and doesn't answer my questions. At first, I was worried that Sienna had some sort of learning disability and would have to be put in a special class.

MOTHER: *(To SIENNA in Filipino—"Did you hear that? They think you're stupid.")* Narinig mo yon. Akala nila tanga ka.

SIENNA: Opo, Nanay. *(Yes, Mother.)*

TEACHER: However, I have noticed that she is farther ahead than the other children in her math skills.

MOTHER: Her father has been teaching her at home.

TEACHER: Well, I am glad that he has taken the initiative. I don't believe that Sienna has a learning disability.

MOTHER: *(To SIENNA in Filipino—"You talk too much at home. Why don't you talk at school?".)* Ang dal-dal mo naman sa bahay! Bakit ang tahimik mo sa eskuwela?

SIENNA: Opo, Nanay.

MOTHER: She will talk more in school.

TEACHER: I think this is the problem. You say that Sienna talks a lot at home.

MOTHER: All the time. She is always telling jokes and stories.

TEACHER: Does she speak in English or in Filipino?

MOTHER: We speak Filipino at home.

TEACHER: I believe that is where the problem lies. I think the language barrier is holding Sienna back from her full potential. She is obviously a very bright and creative girl, as demonstrated in her drawings and mathematical skills, however, she will have great difficulty in the future if this continues.

MOTHER: Is it very bad?

TEACHER: Sienna has no friends in class and she is having great difficulty with the basics of reading and writing. There are no other Filipino children in class and there is no ESL program at this school.

MOTHER: What is there that we can do?

TEACHER: The best thing that you can do for your daughter is to expose her to the English language as much as possible. This means that you must try to speak to her in English while at home. Obviously, there is a language barrier of your own that you and your husband must conquer, but I believe this too can be achieved. Watch English television programs together. Have English conversations. If you are up to it, read to her from English books. This will be a difficult task, but in the end, you will all benefit from this immersion.

MOTHER: Okay, we will do this. Thank you for your help.

TEACHER: You're welcome, and good luck. I hope to see some improvement soon.

MOTHER: Sienna, we are going home.

SIENNA: Opo, Nanay.

MOTHER: No, not Nanay. You call me Mommy from now on. You call me Mommy. Say "Yes, Mommy."

SIENNA: Yes, Mommy.

MOTHER: No more Filipino. English only from now on.

> *Spotlight on SIENNA as MOTHER and TEACHER walk away.*

SIENNA: No more Filipino. English only from now on. Within a couple of years, I was no longer able to speak or understand the Filipino language. They made me into what I am and no one asked if that was okay. Of course, I can't blame them. This was an age before the celebration of diverse multiculturalism. Before political correctness. Before the mosaic. But not before it was too late.

> *Fade out.*

Pinoy Pride

> *Laugh track, spotlight on SIENNA as a standup comedian.*

SIENNA: Hey, I got a good one for you. Did you know Filipinos have a lot of pride? *(In a Filipino accent.)* Pried pish, Pried shrimp, Pried rice.

> *Laugh track.*

How do you say, Uno, Dos, Tres in a sentence? *(In a Filipino accent.)* Oh no, dos trees are burning!

> *Laugh track.*

What's the most times you can use Paul in a sentence? Five.

(In a Filipino accent.) Hey Pol, be care-pol because you might pol in the swimming pol and dat can be bery pain-pol.

> *Laugh track.*

> *Lights up.*

MALAYA: That's not very funny.

SIENNA: Oh, come on. Take a joke. It's funny. Sandy, back me up here.

SANDY: A little funny.

MALAYA: You're making fun of Filipinos.

SIENNA: Just the accent, that's not a big deal.

SANDY: Uh, Sienna. Malaya still has a bit of an accent.

MALAYA: Are you making fun of me?

SIENNA: No, of course not.

MALAYA: So you tell offensive jokes right in front of me and expect me to laugh like the happy little FOB.

SANDY: Whoa, we're taking this a little hard, aren't we Malaya?

SIENNA: They're just jokes. Lighten up.

MALAYA: To you, they're funny, but not to me, not anymore.

            Fade out.

Flip

            Lights up.

SIENNA: Flip.

SANDY: F-L-I-P.

MALAYA: AKA Fucking Little Island Person.

SIENNA: Funky Little Island Person.

SANDY: Freaky Little Island Person.

MALAYA: Frequently Loud Ignorant People.

SIENNA: Fobs Love Ingesting Pets.

SANDY: Foreigners Likely Instigating Problems.

MALAYA: Foreigners Likely Issued Parole.

SIENNA: Funny Language, It's Pilipino!

SANDY: Freaky Loose Immigrant Pussy.

MALAYA: Although I've heard much worse.

Girls face each other.

SIENNA: Fob.

SANDY: Chink.

MALAYA: Jap.

SIENNA: Darkie.

SANDY: Charlie.

MALAYA: Savage.

SIENNA: Chino.

SANDY: Gink.

MALAYA: Jaundy.

SIENNA: Pancake.

SANDY: Nuprin.

MALAYA: Coolie.

SIENNA: Nip.

SANDY: Slanty.

MALAYA: Gook.

SIENNA: Is that all you got? Bring it on!

Circling each other.

SANDY: Dog Eater.

MALAYA: Harbour-Bomber.

SIENNA: Bamboo Coon.

SANDY: Zipper Head.

MALAYA: Rice Picker.

SIENNA: Yellow Nigger.

SANDY: Egg Yolk.

MALAYA: Bug Biter.

SIENNA: Bukakke Warrior.

SANDY: Jungle Girl.

MALAYA: Dim Sum.

SIENNA: Buckethead.

SANDY: Boat People.

MALAYA: Tai Chink.

SIENNA: Hop Sing.

SANDY: Rail Hopper.

MALAYA: Tunnel Digger.

SIENNA: Mail-order bride.

SANDY: Asian Invasion.

MALAYA: Rice Rocketeer.

SIENNA: Slit Slut.

SANDY: Goddamn Flip!

Stop in place.

MALAYA: They're just words.

SANDY: And words only hurt if you let them.

Spotlight on MALAYA.

MALAYA: I'm brown all over, inside and out. Brown eyes, brown skin, brown voice. You can hear it, can't you? The slight accent and the inconsistent grammar that I tried so hard to hide. It comes out, this brown-ness. It's not like I can run away from it. I came here brown and I stayed here brown and I'm stuck with it no matter what I do. It's not like I am fresh. I have been here for over half my life and still they see me as an immigrant. Look at my hands, look at my face. No matter how long I stay here, I'll always be an outsider. I came here when I was young, old enough to amuse them, but not young enough for them to let me in.

               Lights up, two girls wearing white masks approach MALAYA. MALAYA is young with a thick Filipino accent.

GIRL 1:   *(Writing something on a piece of paper, showing it to MALAYA.)* Say this.

MALAYA: Oss-born-ee.

               The girls laugh.

GIRL 2:   What about this?

MALAYA: Asin-boyn-ee.

               The girls laugh more.

GIRL 1:   That's so funny! Malaya, tell her how to get to your house. Go ahead.

MALAYA: I take da bus.

GIRL 1:   No, tell her which bus you take.

MALAYA: Okay, da bus go to da MacPeeleep den to da Jeperson den I go out.

GIRL 1:   Then where?

MALAYA: Den I walk on da Peepeleenee.

GIRL 2:   What did you say? Where did you walk?

MALAYA: Peepeleenee.

GIRL 1:   Pipeline! She meant Pipeline. Peepeleenee.

> *The girls laugh, walking away. MALAYA starts to laugh half-heartedly. Spotlight slowly fades onto MALAYA as laughter dies down.*

MALAYA: I was here two weeks. I was always the center of attention. When I was around, everyone was happy and laughing. On some level I knew they were laughing at me, not with me, but I didn't care because the first day I came here, the kids threw rocks at me and my brother when we walked home from school. And when my brother fought back, they beat him to the ground.

> *Lights up, one kid wearing white mask kicks a sack on the ground, another kid wearing white mask holds MALAYA back.*

MALAYA: Kuya! *(Respectful term for older brother.)*

KID 1:   *(To the brother.)* Come on, Chink. You want to kung fu me? Get up! Get up!

MALAYA: Wag! Tamana! Kuya! Kuya! *(No, stop.)*

KID 1:   You wanna be next?

> *Cross to spotlight on MALAYA.*

MALAYA: If you can't beat them, make them laugh.

> *Lights up on two girls in white masks.*

GIRL 2:   What did you do last weekend?

MALAYA: I bisit my cowsin.

GIRL 1:   You're related to cows?

> *They laugh, walking away.*

MALAYA: I can make you laugh more. If this is the only way
             you will let me in, then laugh. Laugh all you want.
             As long as I can make you laugh, this does not hurt
             me, not in the way you hurt my Kuya.

             Fade out.

Flight of the Tikling Bird

             *Tinikling music plays, lights up, SANDY and
             SIENNA kneel at opposite ends of the parallel
             bamboo poles, MALAYA stands in front of the poles.*

MALAYA: Tinikling: A traditional rural Filipino dance where
             dancers move between bamboo poles. It's a festive
             dance based on the movements of the Tikling bird
             as it moves through the branches of bamboo trees. It
             is the most famous of the Filipino dances, always
             performed at Folklorama and on cultural occasions.

             *Begins to waltz. With grace, the dancer walks
             through bamboo poles. She smiles. She waltzes. She
             dances. She never gets caught.*

             *With skill she dances through the poles as SANDY
             and SIENNA clap the poles to the rhythm. As she
             steps out, clapping stops.*

             I dance for them, because that's what they want.
             That's what they expect. They think they know me.
             They see my brown skin and they hear the accent I
             try so hard to hide. They assume.

             MALAYA turns and takes the place of SIENNA.

             *SIENNA waltzes towards the poles. With grace, the
             dancer flees through the bamboo poles. She avoids
             them. She fears them. She is afraid of being caught.*

             *With awkwardness she dances through the poles as
             SANDY and MALAYA clap the poles. As she steps
             out, clapping stops.*

SIENNA: I dance for them, because that's what they want. That's what they expect. They think they know me. They see my brown skin but they don't think I'm brown enough. They assume.

> *SIENNA takes the place of SANDY.*

> *SANDY waltzes towards the poles. With grace, the dancer glides through the bamboo poles. She challenges. She displays her skill. She dares them to catch her. With confidence she dances through the poles as MALAYA and SIENNA clap the poles. As she steps out, clapping stops.*

SANDY: I dance for them, because that's what they want. That's what they expect. They think they know me. They see my white skin and think that I don't know them. They assume.

> *Music stops, girls stand.*

MALAYA: I'll always be an outsider.

SIENNA: I'll never be the perfect Asian.

SANDY: I'll never be accepted for who I am.

MALAYA: Because of what they expect.

SIENNA: Because they think they know me.

SANDY: Because of what they assume.

MALAYA: But I continue to walk through the poles.

SIENNA: And never get caught.

SANDY: Not because I'm better than them.

MALAYA: Because I have no choice.

> *Fade out.*

The Colour of Her Hair

> *Spotlight on SIENNA.*

SIENNA: When I was young, they used to laugh at me. Maybe because I was chubby, maybe because I was brown. Or maybe because we were all kids and everyone found some reason or other to laugh at each other. I was the only Filipino girl in my class, one of the very few in my school. I stood out like a dark mole on white skin. I always thought they were pointing and laughing. I was surrounded by girls with light coloured eyes, light coloured skin, light coloured hair. I hated them…and envied them at the same time. I longed to be like them, be part of the group. I wanted so badly to blend in. But I had this hair, this flowing black mane that called attention to itself, that branded me as a Filipino, making me stand out. I hated myself then, or at least the colour of my hair.

> *Lights up. MOTHER wears brown mask, has very thick Filipino accent. She is angry that her daughter has run off once again.*

MOTHER: Sienna! Sienna!

SIENNA: I'm coming! What?

MOTHER: K-Mart is very big. You want a bad man to grab you out of the store?

SIENNA: *(Taking her mother's hand.)* No, of course not.

MOTHER: Then you stay here and no running around.

SIENNA: *(Pulling away.)* Mommy, mommy. Can I get chips?

MOTHER: *(Pulling SIENNA back.)* You eat too much. Maybe tomorrow.

SIENNA: But I want chips now!

MOTHER: I buy you chips tomorrow.

SIENNA: Can I have a toy?

MOTHER: Sienna, no toys. It's not your birthday yet. Over
             here. You help me buy the pretty lipstick for the
             christening tomorrow.

SIENNA: Can I wear lipstick?

MOTHER: You are seven years old. You are still a baby. No
             lipstick for you until you grow up.

SIENNA: Yeah, sure.

             Another display catches her eye, her face lights up.

             And then I saw it. I saw all of my dreams come true
             on the cover of a box.

             *A blonde GIRL enters from side wearing white mask,
             posing like a model. She calls to SIENNA.*

GIRL: *(Whispering.)* Sienna…

SIENNA: I walked over, mesmerized by the girl pictured on
             the box.

GIRL: Look at me.

MOTHER: What is that?

GIRL: Love me.

SIENNA: Can we get this? Please?

GIRL: Worship me.

MOTHER: You want this?

GIRL: Covet me.

MOTHER: Hmm, your hair will look pretty like this.

GIRL: You want to be me, don't you?

SIENNA: So you'll buy it?

MOTHER: I buy this for you and you be good and you don't ask
             for nothing more. Okay?

GIRL: And now you can be just like me.

SIENNA: *(Hugging her mother.)* Thank you Mommy! I love
             you Mommy! Thank you!

MOTHER: Hmph.

             SIENNA takes her mother's hand and skips away.

SIENNA: As we walked through the store to make further
             purchases, I beamed. I held on to that box like a
             security blanket. They had to pry it out of my hands
             at the checkout. On the bus I pulled it out of the
             shopping bag and stared at it longingly all the way
             home.

GIRL: You are going to have so much fun when you look
             like me! After all, you know what they say. We do
             have more fun. When you look like me, all the kids
             will like you. All the kids will want to look and be
             like you. No one will laugh at you ever again.

             *GIRL sits on a box, facing the back, her hair
             cascading behind her. SIENNA sits on the floor,
             under GIRL. GIRL's blonde hair is draped over
             SIENNA.*

SIENNA: Blonde. All I ever wanted was to be blonde.
             Suzanne Sommers was blonde. Farrah Fawcett was
             blonde. Barbie was blonde. Even Smurfette was
             blonde. Blonde, because blonde is pretty. Blonde is
             fun…

GIRL: *(Joining in.)* Blonde is fun. Blonde is perfect and the
             epitome of what any girl could ever want.

SIENNA: I was so happy when we got home. I ran to the
             mirror and put the box of hair solution next to my
             own image, fantasizing about what I was going to
             look like.

GIRL: *(Turning around, putting her face next to SIENNA's.)*
             We're like sisters, like the Wakefield twins and the
             Brady Bunch.

SIENNA: You think so?

GIRL: You'll finally fit it. You'll finally be one of us.

SIENNA: Mommy, Mommy! Can we do this now? Can we fix my hair now?

MOTHER: Later.

SIENNA: We won't have time tomorrow and I want to look pretty for the party.

MOTHER: Hmm, okay. You change, I get my things.

SIENNA: Yay! It's happening! It's finally happening!

              SIENNA sits as her mother begins to prep her hair.

              I watched closely as my mother carefully measured out the ingredients, pouring and mixing and shaking and squeezing. She began to apply the solution to my hair, her fingers working their magic. I continued to gaze at the box.

GIRL: Soon, you'll be beautiful and perfect, just like me.

SIENNA: Beautiful and perfect.

MOTHER: Are you talking to me?

SIENNA: Thank you Mommy. Thank you for making me beautiful and perfect.

MOTHER: Hmph.

SIENNA: When she finished, she wrapped my hair up into a towel and told me to wait an hour. The smell made me nauseated, the fumes made my eyes sting and the chemicals burned into my scalp. I gritted my teeth through the pain and thought of the process that the caterpillar went through on her way to becoming a butterfly.

GIRL: A beautiful and perfect blonde butterfly.

SIENNA: I awaited my transformation.

MOTHER: Sienna! Is time! I have to rinse your hair. Come here. Close your eyes.

             MOTHER takes towel off, taking everything out of SIENNA's hair. SIENNA closes her eyes tightly.

SIENNA: As I felt the cool water rinse the black ugliness away, I pictured the caterpillar emerging, seeing the world through new eyes, realizing she can finally fly away from everyone.

GIRL: Open your eyes Sienna. Look at your loveliness.

MOTHER: Open. Look in the mirror. It's so pretty.

             Pause.

SIENNA: In one instant, all my dreams of achieving perfection had been dashed against the rocks of reality. I wasn't pretty. I wasn't perfect. I wasn't blonde. How could I be so stupid? It was a box of perming solution, not hair colour. All I saw was the blonde hair of the girl on the box. I never even bothered to see that her hair was curly.

GIRL: Poor little Sienna. No matter how hard you try, you can never look like me. You'll never be me.

SIENNA: All I saw was me, ugly, dirty, black-haired me.

GIRL: You will never fit in. You will never be one of us.

MOTHER: Sienna? You don't like? Sienna?

SIENNA: I tore up the box, although I could still hear her laughing. I heard everyone laughing.

GIRL: *(Walking away.)* Poor little dark-haired Sienna.

SIENNA: I threw myself onto my bed and for an hour, I cried, drying my tears into my ugly, dirty, black and curly hair.

             Fade out.

Chicken Nut Bread

> *Laugh track, spotlight on SIENNA as standup comedian.*

SIENNA: Why is there no Disneyland in the Philippines? No one is tall enough to go on the good rides.

> *Laugh track.*

Why do Filipino guys drive low-riders? So they can drive and pick rice at the same time.

> *Laugh track.*

While getting off the plane, a Filipino gets stopped by immigration. They tell him, "We need to test out your English skills. Use the words, Chicken, Nut and Bread in a sentence." The Filipino looks around, puts a plastic bag over a woman's head and yells "Chee can not breed! Chee can not breed!"

> *Laugh track.*

> *Lights up.*

MALAYA: Now those weren't funny at all.

SIENNA: Yes, they are. Get over it, Malaya.

SANDY: You're reaching, Sienna.

MALAYA: I thought you were tired of being laughed at.

SIENNA: It's just a joke.

MALAYA: You told me about how they used to laugh at you. You told me how you hated it.

SIENNA: I did… I still do.

MALAYA: Then why give them something to laugh at?

> *Fade out.*

Funny Language, It's Pilipino!

> *Sound of overlapping Filipino voices, lights up, fade sound down.*

SIENNA: Blah blah blah. It all sounds the same to me now. I'm told that when I was little, I was fluent, but now, I don't get any of it. Sure, I can pick out some, but no, I don't understand. Not anymore. Not that it makes a difference.

> *A FILIPINO woman enters, wearing a brown mask.*

FILIPINO: Sienna, ano gusto mong inumin? *(What would you like to drink?)*

SIENNA: Pardon?

FILIPINO: Ano gusto mong inumin?

SIENNA: I'm sorry. I don't understand.

FILIPINO: You don't know Talalog?

SIENNA: No, just a little. Usually whatever my mother is saying, but that's about it.

FILIPINO: You are born here.

SIENNA: Yes.

FILIPINO: And your parents never teach you?

SIENNA: Yes, they did, but I've forgotten. We speak English in my house. So, what were you asking me?

FILIPINO: Oh, what would you like to drink?

SIENNA: They look at me and see Filipino scrawled all over my face. Surely she speaks it... But it really pisses me off when there are two Filipinos standing right in front of me, with the full knowledge that I have no idea what they're saying.

> *Two giggly Filipino GIRLS sit to the side, both wearing brown masks, translation later in scene.*

GIRL 1:   Bumili ako ng kamesita.

GIRL 2:   Ano ang itsura?

GIRL 1:   Kapareho ng kulay ng suhot ni Sienna.

Laughter.

GIRL 2:   Laging yan ang kulay na suhot mo.

GIRL 1:   Tama ka!

Laughter.

SIENNA: Half the time, I think they're talking about me.

Repeat same scene in English.

GIRL 1:   I bought a new shirt.

GIRL 2:   Really? What does it look like?

GIRL 1:   It's the same colour as what Sienna is wearing.

Laughter.

GIRL 2:   You always wear the same colour.

GIRL 1:   I think you're right!

Laughter, girls walk away.

SIENNA: Okay, maybe I'm paranoid. Not everyone is talking about me. Not all the time.

SIENNA walks away, MALAYA takes her place.

MALAYA: Ang laging kong salita ay Tagalog. Mas madali kay sa English. *(I usually speak Tagalog. It's easier than English.)*

A GIRL with a white mask enters.

WHITE GIRL: *(Snotty.)* Why do those Fobs have to keep talking in their own language? It's just so rude. I mean, we're in Canada. We speak English here.

MALAYA: English is my second language. In other words, my first language is Filipino. I grew up speaking Filipino. My thoughts are in Filipino.

WHITE GIRL: Hey, Fob. Try taking some ESL.

MALAYA: English as a Superior Language? No thank you.

WHITE GIRL: Go home, Jungle Girl.

MALAYA: I am home, Canuck Girl. There's so much that I want to say, but I can't get the words out, not in English. It's not fair that I understand you and I can't talk back. I can't fight. I don't have the words.

WHITE GIRL: You have something to say?

MALAYA: *(Turning to GIRL, smiling sweetly.)* Putang ina mo. *(Equivalent to "Fuck You".)*

WHITE GIRL: What did you say?

MALAYA: *(In a thick accent.)* Hab a good day!

               Turns away from the girl, speaking normally.

               All my life, I have been surrounded by the Filipino language. Why would that change the moment I step off the plane? Or off the boat as some may think.

               Two Filipino women wearing brown masks enter, start talking to each other in low voices, pointing at SANDY, translation later in scene.

WOMAN 1:   Yan ba ang nobya ng anak mo.

WOMAN 2:   Gusto lang niya ng puti na malande.

WOMAN 1:   Sana hindi sha mabuntis.

WOMAN 2:   Ayo ko ng ma nga apo na mestiso.

SANDY: All my life, I've been surrounded by Filipino. Yes, the pasty skin is a dead giveaway, isn't it? I picked up some here and there from friends and neighbours, but most of it came from listening, and I mean really listening carefully. Unfortunately, I understand what they are saying. For those who don't...

WOMAN 1:   Yan ba ang nobya ng anak mo.

SANDY: Is that your son's girlfriend?

WOMAN 2:   Gusto lang niya ng puti na malande.

SANDY: He only likes white sluts.

WOMAN 1:   Sana hindi sha mabuntis.

SANDY: Hopefully she won't get pregnant.

WOMAN 2:   Ayo ko ng ma nga apo na mestiso.

SANDY: I don't want half-breed grandchildren.

SANDY, MALAYA, and SIENNA stand.

I'm not allowed to defend myself because I'm not supposed to understand.

MALAYA: I want to be free to speak my language, to think my language. This is the only way I can understand.

SIENNA: I'll never understand.

Fade out.

Somewhere Over the Ocean

Sound of an airplane flying overhead. Center spotlight. Person in center wearing half-brown/half-white mask, plays all other characters in scene.

A FLIGHT ATTENDANT explains procedure to passengers.

FLIGHT
ATTENDANT: The exits are indicated as follows, two doors at the

front, two doors at the rear and two exits over the wings. In the event of depressurization of the cabin, oxygen masks will fall from directly in front of you. If this should occur, place the mask over your mouth and nose and breath normally. In the event of a water evacuation, life vests are located underneath your seats. Enjoy your flight and thank you for flying Cathay Pacific.

Two spotlights on SIENNA and MALAYA on either side.

SIENNA: December.

MALAYA: 1989.

SIENNA: My parents took me to the Philippines.

MALAYA: Me and my brother left the Philippines.

BOTH: I was only twelve.

SIENNA: We were going to celebrate Christmas in their homeland.

MALAYA: I would see the new year in my new home country.

NEWSCASTER: In the news today…Makati, Manila: A failed coup attempt has been made against the Philippine president, Corazon Aquino. A reward of one million pesos, equivalent to fifty thousand dollars US funds, has been offered for information leading to the arrest and capture of those involved. Sources say that the coup d'etat was funded by former Philippine first lady Imelda Marcos, in hopes of regaining her seat in power.

SIENNA: Maybe not the best timing to go there.

MALAYA: It was a perfect time to leave.

SIENNA: The country was in turmoil.

MALAYA: My mother wanted me safe.

BOTH: It was the first time I rode in an airplane.

SIENNA: I was so…

MALAYA: Scared.

SIENNA: Not of crashing into the sea.

MALAYA: Meeting my family.

SIENNA: We had a stopover in Japan.

MALAYA: The sky was red.

SIENNA: Seven hours.

MALAYA: I watched the sunset.

SIENNA: It was the most beautiful thing I had ever seen.

BOTH: When I stepped off the plane…

SIENNA: In the Philippines.

MALAYA: In Canada.

SIENNA: There was a woman waiting.

MALAYA: She smiled and said…

WOMAN: Welcome.

SIENNA: And I thought…

MALAYA: Maybe this isn't so scary after all.

SIENNA: We had to register at the embassy.

MALAYA: I had to speak to immigration.

WOMAN: I will need to see your passport and identification.

SIENNA: My parents signed documents.

MALAYA: They took my picture.

WOMAN: Thank you, and I hope you enjoy your time here.

SIENNA: We rode on a bus for four hours to reach Gimba.

MALAYA: My aunt and uncle…my new parents drove us to their home.

DRIVER: *(With Filipino accent.)* You will like it here, you'll see.

SIENNA: I couldn't believe the heat, thirty-two degrees Celsius in the middle of winter.

MALAYA: I had never seen snow before.

SIENNA: It was so hot. My skin itched. I took my jacket off. I changed to spandex bicycle shorts and a t-shirt that had a peace symbol on the front. My skin was so pale.

MALAYA: I never knew how cold it was. When I stepped out of the car, I reached down, putting my hands into the snow. I brought it up to my face to smell it. My face got wet. I couldn't feel my fingers.

MERCHANT: Siopao! Lechon!

SIENNA: The bus would stop and merchants would ride with us to the next town. They would sell magazines and snacks.

MALAYA: They prepared rice and fish and adobo and pancit. I never ate so much at one time. I got a little sick.

SIENNA: I read about the coup, how unhappy people were.

MALAYA: I had been without for so long. It was strange to have so much.

NEWSCASTER: In the news today…Makati, Manila: Protesters flock into the streets outside the presidential palace, demanding action be taken towards the current economic recession. President Corazon Aquino is currently on a worldwide mission searching for investment in the Philippine economy as well as debt reconciliation.

SIENNA: They thought after the revolution everything would change, get better.

MALAYA: My family could not take care of us, so they sent us here, where we would never starve.

SIENNA: I began to understand why my mother left home.

MALAYA: I missed my home.

SIENNA: I stepped off the bus.

MALAYA: My first day of school.

SIENNA: I was nervous about meeting my cousins and aunts and uncles...

MALAYA: New classmates. Maybe new friends.

SIENNA: Meeting my grandmother for the first time.

MALAYA: The teacher asked me to stand at the front of my class.

SIENNA: I smiled. I said "Hello. I'm Sienna."

MALAYA: "I am named Malaya."

SIENNA: One of my cousins—I don't remember which one—said to her mother...

GIRL: Bakit siya mataba?

SIENNA: "Why is she so fat?"

GIRL: "FOB!"

MALAYA: A girl called out. The class laughed. The teacher told me to sit down.

BOTH: I wanted to go back home.

SIENNA: They kept staring at me.

MALAYA: They were whispering to each other.

SIENNA: Talking about me.

MALAYA: Calling me names.

SIENNA: Pointing.

MALAYA: Laughing.

SIENNA: In front of my face.

MALAYA: Like I wasn't even there.

BOTH: I couldn't understand what they were saying.

SIENNA: So I smiled.

MALAYA: And nodded.

SIENNA: Because I was young.

MALAYA: And I didn't know any better.

SIENNA: Later that day.

MALAYA: They had the nerve to ask.

GIRL: I need a favour.

BOTH: Yes?

COUSIN: *(With Filipino accent.)* Sienna, you're from America.

SIENNA: Canada, actually.

GIRL: Malaya, you're Oriental.

MALAYA: I am Filipino.

COUSIN: *(With Filipino accent.)* You are rich.

SIENNA: You want me to give you money?

GIRL: You're good at math.

MALAYA: You want to cheat off me?

                    MALAYA and SIENNA laugh.

SIENNA: I don't think so.

MALAYA: Are you kidding?

> *GIRL walks away.*

SIENNA: I'm older.

MALAYA: And wiser now.

SIENNA: I don't care what they assume.

MALAYA: I don't care if they laugh.

BOTH: But I won't give in to them.

SIENNA: I won't give in to their assumptions.

MALAYA: I won't give in to their ignorance.

SIENNA: I know better than that.

MALAYA: I know better than them.

BOTH: They don't know me at all.

> *Fade out.*

You Know You're a Filipino if...

> *Lights up.*

ALL: You know you're a Filipino if...

SIENNA: You have rice stuck to the front of your shirt.

SANDY: You eat rice with everything, including KFC.

MALAYA: Because rice with anything is a perfect meal.

SIENNA: You know you're a Filipino if you wear tsnelas, or slippers, around your house.

SANDY: Your furniture is covered in plastic.

MALAYA: Your carpet is covered in plastic.

SIENNA: And yet you continue to wear tsnelas around the house.

SANDY: You know you're a Filipino if you point with your lips.

MALAYA: You greet people with a nod.

SIENNA: And raised eyebrows.

SANDY: Don't forget the obligatory hiss.

MALAYA: *(Does all of the above: nods, points with lips, raises eyebrows, hisses.)* Psst.

SIENNA: You've got to be a Filipino if your name is Tito Boy, Ate Girlie or Lola Baby.

SANDY: Your parents call you Nic-Nic, Che-Che or Lyn-Lyn.

MALAYA: You know you're a Filipino if you have a giant fork and spoon in your kitchen.

SIENNA: A shield displaying the Weapons of Moroland hangs in the living room.

SANDY: A laughing Buddha sits underneath it.

MALAYA: And the paint of his belly is faded from people rubbing it for luck.

SIENNA: You have a rock in the bathtub.

SANDY: And don't ask what it's for.

MALAYA: You have a small bucket on the toilet.

SIENNA: Don't ask what it's for.

SANDY: You have a statue of a man in a barrel on top of the piano that no one plays.

MALAYA: Trust me, don't lift up the barrel.

SIENNA: Schwing!

SANDY: You know you're a Filipino if you eat dinuguan.

MALAYA: Also known as 'Chocolate Meat'.

SIENNA: But trust me, it's not chocolate.

SANDY: And balot is your favourite snack.

MALAYA: But you try not to think of the aborted duck fetus
              while you eat it.

              All three girls cringe.

SIENNA: You have found creative ways of cooking corned
              beef and Spam.

SANDY: You put Vienna sausages in your spaghetti.

MALAYA: And you still eat it with a side of rice.

SIENNA: Everyone asks you to invite them over when you're
              serving up a batch of pancit.

SANDY: With your special barbecue pork shishkabobs with
              the secret 7-Up marinade.

MALAYA: You know you're a Filipino if your mother is a
              seamstress, a nurse or a domestic worker.

SIENNA: Your father works for Boeing, CN or CP Rail.

SANDY: Combined, they work over a hundred hours a week

MALAYA: Even if it means you're raised by your Lola.

SIENNA: And you wear hand-me-downs.

SANDY: And they don't take you to movies.

MALAYA: Or special dinners.

SIENNA: They came here for a better life for you.

SANDY: Leaving everything they knew behind.

MALAYA: Even though they gross over eighty thousand per
              year, they keep the smaller house.

SIENNA: They scrimp.

SANDY: They save.

MALAYA: They sacrifice.

SIENNA: To send you to university.

SANDY: Because they want for you what they couldn't have.

MALAYA: And yes, you may be angry.

SIENNA: Because they weren't always there.

SANDY: They couldn't give you that trip to Europe.

MALAYA: Or that new car.

SIENNA: Instead, they give you a chance for a better life.

SANDY: Even if you will never know what they had left behind.

MALAYA: You know you're a Filipino if your parents have done everything in their power to give you everything that you need.

SIENNA: Be proud to be a Filipino.

SANDY: Even if you are kind of quirky with the rice and the bucket and the barrel man.

MALAYA: Thank you Mom.

SIENNA: Thank you Dad.

ALL: Thank you for giving me pride.

                Fade out.

Sew What?

                Sound of sewing machines, three spotlights, SIENNA and MALAYA on sides, sewing, WOMAN in center wearing white mask.

SIENNA: Recruiters from Holland came to the Philippines in the mid-sixties, looking for seamstresses to work in garment factories.

WOMAN: Come one! Come all! Young Filipina women, we offer you the chance of a lifetime! Be a part of our team in Holland. Yes, Holland, the place with the windmills and the wooden shoes. On the other side of the world, in the heart of Europe. We offer you a ticket, a room, a job and a wage. All we ask is that you sew a straight line. Help your families. See the world! Join us in Holland!

SIENNA: My mother was part of the Wehl group, arriving in Holland in 1967. Later in the sixties, garment factories in Canada began making similar offers, particularly to those who had just returned from their terms in Holland. Winnipeg was one of the hubs of the industry.

WOMAN: Come one! Come all! Young Filipina women, we offer you the chance of a lifetime! Be a part of our team in Winnipeg…Canada. On the other side of the world, right above America. We offer you a job and the English language. Sponsor your families. See the snow! Join us in Winnipeg!

SIENNA: Filipina women immigrated to Canada, settling in Winnipeg. Over the years, they brought their families, had children.

WOMAN: Come to Canada. Sew in our factories. Pay our taxes. Educate your children. Our arms are open wide.

MALAYA: And now there are over fifty thousand Filipinos in Winnipeg, hundreds of thousands of Filipinos in Canada… And still we are considered outsiders.

> *Lights up, WOMAN wearing white mask sitting on bench, MALAYA approaches, sits on the bench. The WOMAN gives her a dirty look and stands up. A man wearing white mask approaches. He looks at the bench. Decides to stand next to the WOMAN. MALAYA checks her watch, looks for bus. Stands up. MAN and WOMAN sit down.*

WOMAN: My son was laid off last year. Too many immigrants were hired at the factory.

MAN: It's because they take lower wages. Rather than paying an honest man some honest money, they'd rather save a buck and give it to some poor schmuck that fell off a boat.

WOMAN: A Filipino family moved into a house just down my street. Two months later, three other Filipino families moved into the area.

MAN: They're probably all related.

WOMAN: Tell me about it. The property value of my house has dropped drastically since those people moved in.

MAN: Are there gangs in your area too?

WOMAN: I always see them hanging around the corner store. I think they're selling drugs. Some of the girls look like they're practicing to be prostitutes.

MALAYA: Maybe they think I don't understand English.

WOMAN: They steal our jobs.

MAN: And they date our sons.

WOMAN: That's where all these half-breed children are coming from, born from all these fourteen-year-old girls.

MAN: I've heard they don't have birth control in Asia, that it's illegal to use contraception.

WOMAN: That's probably why these Oriental girls are so loose.

MALAYA: Or maybe they're just ignorant.

MAN: Many of these Filipinos are taking on two or more jobs. That's why the unemployment is so high.

WOMAN: They take all the jobs. There's nothing left for us Canadians.

MAN: They come from these countries where all they have to eat is rice and once they get here, boom, they want it all. Two cars, a big house—

WOMAN: They move into the suburbs and ruin it for people who've lived here all their lives.

MAN: Why can't they stay in the central part of the city, with their own kind?

MALAYA: But I say nothing. What can I say? Am I supposed to tell them that we end up working the jobs that no one else wants? That the minimum wage of one job isn't enough to pay for rent and food? That we work hard to get out of the slums and into more affluent areas to get away from the gangs?

WOMAN: Ah, our bus is here.

              The MAN and WOMAN stand up, boarding the bus.

MALAYA: I say nothing. I still can't find the words. I've been here for years. I know what I should say. I have worked on my diction. I have worked on my accent. I have worked on my pronunciation, but still I can't say it. I can't find the right words to say. So I say nothing. Because I'm afraid they won't listen. Because I'm afraid it won't make a difference. Because I'm still afraid of them.

              Looks at the bus driver.

              Thanks, I'll catch the next one.

              Sits down, waits. SANDY enters from back.

SANDY: There was a girl at the bus stop the other day. I was walking up and I heard these people saying these terrible things.

MAN goes back to place on bench.

MAN: It's because they take lower wages. Rather than paying an honest man some honest money, they'd rather save a buck and give it to some poor schmuck that fell off a boat.

SANDY: What a load of bullshit. I wanted to go right up to them and scream at them. What is wrong with you?

MAN: Why can't they stay in the central part of the city, with their own kind?

SANDY: But I look down at my hands, at my pasty skin. I'm not Filipino. I'm an "Honourary Filipino". When I'm with my friends, that's one thing. But no one else understands. What right do I have to say anything?

MAN: Great, another politically correct save the minorities love the world wannabe-coloured anti-racism crusader. Spare me.

SANDY: And what if this girl gets mad at me if I try to defend her?

MALAYA: Who the hell do you think you are? I can take care of myself, white girl. Step off and mind your own business.

SANDY: So I say nothing. Because I don't know if I have the right. Or maybe I'm just afraid it won't make any difference at all.

          Fade out.

Balancing Skills

> *Binasuan music starts. Lights up. SIENNA and SANDY stand with glasses on their hands. If capable, they should dance balancing glasses on their heads. They begin to waltz. MALAYA steps forward.*

MALAYA: Binasuan: A colourful and lively dance displaying the balancing skills of the dancers. The glasses that the dancers gracefully, yet carefully, maneuver are normally half-filled with rice wine. Binasuan, meaning "with the use of a drinking glass", is often performed as entertainment at weddings, birthdays, and fiestas.

SIENNA: It's all about balance.

SANDY: Friends.

SIENNA: Boys.

SANDY: To each their own.

SIENNA: I date white guys.

SANDY: I date Asians.

SIENNA: It's not that I don't like Filipino guys.

SANDY: It's not that I don't like white guys.

BOTH: This is all I know.

SIENNA: My friends are white.

SANDY: My friends are Asian.

BOTH: So what kind of guys do I meet?

> *Music stops, girls stop dancing, spotlights on both girls.*

SIENNA: *(Twisting glass in her hand, raising it above her head.)* I used to like Filipino guys. In grade six, another

Filipino boy arrived at our school. I was so happy. Finally, I wasn't the only one. Other than family gatherings where I was related to everyone, I didn't know many Filipino guys. His name was Rhomar—a combination of his parents, Rhonda and Mario. He had spiky hair and wore sweater vests. He was a preppy and really cute. We were the only Filipinos so everyone in class started to bug us. Sienna and Rhomar, Sienna and Rhomar... They started combining our names. Sien-Mar or Rho-na. I asked to dance with him at the next school dance. He walked away.

SANDY: *(Twisting glass in her hand, raising it above her head.)* The first boy who asked me out was a Chinese boy, the one who owned the restaurant three blocks away from the school. We went out once. But the next day it was all over school. In my multicultural inner city junior high, you'd think people would be a little more open, but that wasn't quite the case. A few days later, someone vandalized my locker. They spray painted C-O-C-K-A-S-I-A-N... Cock-Asian. I only went out with him once. That year, no one asked me out again.

Girls put glasses down.

SIENNA: I was attracted to Filipinos, but it never came back to me. When I began to meet other Filipino guys my age, they would always look at the other Asian girls with the petite bodies and Hello Kitty cell phones. How am I supposed to compete with that?

SANDY: All of my friends were Asian. I met my friends' friends and their friends and I felt comfortable with them. I didn't see the differences between us at all. I mean, let's be real. White, red, yellow, black, we're all just shades of brown.

SIENNA: I've only dated white guys, not because of preference, but because of availability. No Filipino has ever asked me out. If someone does, hey, I'm game, but I must admit that I have a thing for blue eyes. Show me a Filipino with baby blue eyes—real baby blue eyes, not contacts—and I just may melt.

SANDY: I do admit that I like shorter guys. I don't like straining my neck. Without the aid of front porch steps, that kiss goodnight is really tricky. But a shorter guy, I can wrap my arms around him and feel…equal.

BOTH: But some people don't understand.

> *Lights up, FLIP MOM in center wearing half-brown/half-white mask. She speaks with accent.*

FLIP MOM: He's white.

SIENNA: Yes, he's white.

WHITE MOM: An Oriental?

SANDY: Filipino actually.

FLIP MOM: Why don't you go with a Filipino boy?

SIENNA: I like white guys.

WHITE MOM: Another Asian?

SANDY: What's wrong with Asians?

FLIP MOM: Your aunties know lots of Filipino boys.

SIENNA: I'm dating someone.

WHITE MOM: What's wrong with dating your own kind?

SANDY: I date who I date.

FLIP MOM: I don't like this boy.

BOTH: You don't even know him!

SANDY: Oh wait, it gets better.

WHITE MOM: Mrs. Schultz down the street has a nice grandson.

SANDY: And I suppose he's nice and WASPy?

WHITE MOM: He's not Portuguese, but I can settle.

SIENNA: That's nothing.

FLIP MOM: Your auntie knows a boy in the Philippines. You can be his pen pal.

SIENNA: So that we can fall madly in love and I can sponsor him over and he can get free health care? No thanks.

SANDY: Is that all you got?

WHITE MOM: What are other people going to think?

SANDY: I don't care what they think.

WHITE MOM: I just don't want people thinking less of you.

SANDY: And why would anyone think that?

SIENNA: I can do even better.

FLIP MOM: Mestisa babies are very beautiful, but that doesn't mean you have to make one for yourself.

SIENNA: I've gone out with him twice.

SANDY: Oh yeah?

WHITE MOM: He's too dark for you.

SIENNA: Really?

                The girls pick up the glasses, Binasuan music fades in, girls begin to dance, spinning.

FLIP MOM: You're too dark for him.

WHITE MOM: You should meet more friends your own colour.

FLIP MOM: If you came out with us to more parties, you'd meet more pinoys.

WHITE MOM: Our cleaning staff at work is Filipino.

FLIP MOM: He will treat you like a maid.

WHITE MOM: Of course, I'm not prejudiced or anything.

FLIP MOM: Some white people are very nice, but not all of them.

WHITE MOM: But why do you have to be so politically correct?

FLIP MOM: But I don't like him for you.

SANDY/SIENNA: MOM!

> *Girls drop glasses, music stops.*
>
> *Fade out.*

Legend of the Asian Princess

> *Muslim gongs play. Spotlight on MALAYA holding elaborately decorated fans, she wears a string of bells at her ankle and stands in position for the Singkil dance as the Asian princess. SIENNA and SANDY kneel at ends of bamboo poles, heads bowed low.*

MALAYA: Singkil—A royal dance originating in the southern Muslim area of the Philippines still practiced today. The dance is based on an ancient legend of a princess who had been caught in an earthquake caused by fairies of the forest. Crisscrossed bamboo poles represent fallen trees and fan dancers represent the fairies. Muslim princesses to this day are taught this noble and beautiful dance.

> *MALAYA begins to dance through poles. SANDY and SIENNA are the clappers. Singkil clappers keep their heads bowed low. Please note, the 'music' for this dance comes from the clapping of the poles. At the end, MALAYA stands in an angled position with fans, clapping stops.*

The Asian princess. She is lovely, exotic, and graceful. She is demure. She lowers her eyes. She takes small steps with her tiny feet. Her mouth is small and never opens. She is well-behaved. She never talks back. She is disciplined, intelligent and practical.

> *SIENNA and SANDY stand. They hold fans and stand in the same regal position. Singkil music begins, all three dance.*

SIENNA: She wears clothes from the Gap, Club Monaco and Tommy Hilfigger.

SANDY: She smells like Calvin Klein and wears a belly button ring.

MALAYA: Her shirts show off her midriff and her jeans show off slender ankles.

SIENNA: She has clunky shoes with thick soles that add three inches to her height.

SANDY: She wears dark lipstick and over-accentuates her eyes with black eyeliner.

MALAYA: She is covered in subtle swipes of body glitter.

SIENNA: She dyes her hair copper and her skin is not too dark.

SANDY: She's good at math and wants to be a nurse when she grows up.

MALAYA: She likes to listen to rap and hip hop and loves to sing karaoke.

> *They drop the fans, music stops, they stand normally.*

SIENNA: An Asian woman is proud.

SANDY: She holds her head up.

MALAYA: And she doesn't take shit from anyone.

> *Lights up. MALAYA sits across from her guidance counsellor who wears a white mask.*

COUNSELLOR: An actor.

MALAYA: Yes, an actor.

COUNSELLOR: You want to be an actor.

MALAYA: I just need help choosing my courses.

COUNSELLOR: I thought you wanted to be a nurse or an engineer.

MALAYA: I never said I wanted that.

COUNSELLOR: With your grades, you could easily be accepted in the faculty of science.

MALAYA: I have a lot of difficulties with math.

COUNSELLOR: You would easily fit in with the computer science and pre-med students.

MALAYA: I want to be an actor. Acting comes natural to me. I enjoy performing and being on the stage.

COUNSELLOR: I realize that you have played the lead role in the annual school musical for the last three years, but that doesn't mean that you should pursue a career in this field.

MALAYA: Last summer, I started singing for weddings and debuts and I've already tried auditioning for local roles.

COUNSELLOR: It's wonderful for you to take up a hobby, but as your guidance counsellor it's my job to guide you in decisions that will affect your future. I want to help you.

MALAYA: Then what's wrong with my choice?

COUNSELLOR: You are a very talented girl, Malaya, however the world of performing arts is extremely competitive. For someone of your...race, there is very little that this world can offer. If you were black or white, or even of Aboriginal descent, there might be more opportunities out there but for someone like you the odds are almost impossible.

MALAYA: Because I'm Asian?

COUNSELLOR: I'm going to give you some pamphlets about science and nursing. Please look them over and make an informed decision.

MALAYA: *(Standing up.)* If it's all the same to you, I've already heard enough to make a decision on my own.

> *Spotlight on MALAYA, picks up fans, poses, music begins again.*

> The Asian princess is graceful and beautiful and intelligent and cunning and resourceful. Nothing stands in her way.

> *Begins to dance.*

> I'll show them that the Asian princess can do anything she puts her mind to, whether it's dodging trees or becoming an actor. I am a lot stronger than they think.

> *Fade out.*

Another Night at the Debut

> *Lights up. Asian Cha Cha music starts. All three girls begin to cha cha.*

MALAYA: The Debut: The party of all parties to celebrate the eighteenth birthday of a Filipina girl.

SANDY: A lavish extravaganza to introduce the Debutante to the world.

SIENNA: An over-priced party to sell your daughter.

MALAYA/
SANDY: *(Stop dancing.)* Sienna!

SIENNA: I call it as I see it.

                Start dancing again.

MALAYA: Months of preparation, comparable to that of a wedding.

SANDY: Three dresses or more, for the introduction, for the dinner, for the dance.

SIENNA: And then there's the cotillion. The Debutante picks out her closest friends and puts them through a horrid nightmare of waltzes, cha chas and a tame form of the lambada.

MALAYA: They're not that bad.

                Music fades out.

SIENNA: I'm sorry, but this is *not* my scene.

                Country music starts, spotlight on SIENNA.

                I went to a social in Lorette with friends I met in school. Rural town socials are the best. Best food, best music, and best of all, no pressure.

                I was the only brown girl there. I stood out, but it wasn't in a bad way. Everyone was dancing and having fun. For once, I didn't feel like a blimp. Of course I didn't think I was this exotic Asian goddess that would sweep in and become the center of attention. I was just a girl, among many girls. For once, I wasn't the heaviest girl in the room. No one called me fat. I was just Sienna, this Filipino girl who didn't have to be taught the electric slide.

                BOY wearing white mask enters, holds out his hand, dances the two step with SIENNA as she continues speaking.

                A guy asked me to dance. He taught me the two step. I was sixteen, he was eighteen. We danced most of the night to cheesy country songs and we exchanged numbers and started dating. My cousin had a debut a month later, held at one of the restaurants that serve Filipino cuisine. Of course I asked him to be my date.

BOY pulls out chair for SIENNA.

BOY: Wow, it's so extravagant.

SIENNA: Some people are of the mindset, the bigger the better.

BOY: Wasn't she wearing something different ten minutes ago?

SIENNA: That was the dress for the entrance. She's wearing a dinner dress now.

BOY: So when is this fancy dance?

SIENNA: They perform after dinner. It's a lot of bells and whistles. I'm sorry I dragged you to this.

BOY: No, I want to learn more about you and your culture.

SIENNA: Well, this isn't really me, but I guess it's a cultural thing.

AUNT enters wearing brown mask.

AUNT: Hoy!

SIENNA: Oh no.

BOY: What?

AUNT: Sienna!

SIENNA: Hello, Auntie Baby.

AUNT: You stand up. You are so big!

SIENNA: I've always been tall, Auntie Baby.

AUNT: If you lose a little weight, you would be so beautiful.

BOY: I think she's beautiful just the way she is.

AUNT: You must be Sienna's new boyfriend. You are from the country, right?

BOY: From Lorette, Ma'am.

AUNT: Where's your cowboy hat?

SIENNA: He's not from Texas, Auntie Baby.

AUNT: You two will have such beautiful mestisa babies.

SIENNA: I'm only sixteen.

AUNT: You are a good girl, Sienna. I will see you later. *(Exits.)*

SIENNA: I'm so sorry about that.

BOY: No, it's okay. That was kind of funny.

SIENNA: Yeah, funny.

BOY: So, tell me, what is everything?

SIENNA: Well, I don't exactly know what it's all called, but I do know that this is pork with some sort of sauce and this is some sort of eggroll. This is called pancit.

BOY: That I knew.

AUNT: *(Approaching them.)* How is everything?

SIENNA: Everything is fine, Auntie Baby.

AUNT: Don't eat too much, Sienna. You want to lose weight, right?

SIENNA: Whatever you say, Auntie Baby.

AUNT: *(To BOY.)* You don't like?

BOY: I haven't really had a chance to try anything yet.

AUNT: Do you need ketchup? I will get ketchup. Psst! *(Waving to unseen server.)*

SIENNA: Auntie Baby, we're fine. Look, someone's calling you over. I think someone's about to sing.

AUNT: I will see you later! Don't eat the lechon, Sienna. Pork is very bad for you.

            AUNT exits. SIENNA looks down at her food.

SIENNA: Screw this. Can we just go?

BOY: I'm fine, Sienna.

SIENNA: But I'm not. I don't want to be here anymore. I can't deal with this.

BOY: Okay, we'll go.

            They get up to leave.

            Spotlight on SIENNA.

SIENNA: We dated a month or two more. I stopped bringing boyfriends to Debuts and Filipino socials. I was so embarrassed of my family. So I stopped bringing boys home. I couldn't defend them. I couldn't defend myself. I didn't know what to do or what to say. Maybe someday I'll find the words.

            Fade out.

            Spotlight on SANDY entering, she waves to people she knows, she sits down.

SANDY: Who put ketchup on the table? Ha, Ha, very funny. I'll bring you soy sauce for your shepherd's pie the next time you come over for dinner.

            Dance music, chase lights, SANDY catches the rhythm and stands up.

            I went to plenty of debuts in my time. I was even involved in a few, as a candle lighter, and I was even in a cotillion. I never got into socials, but debuts, that was definitely my scene. I'd walk in, say hi to a few friends, work the room and eventually make my way to the dance floor. They say white girls can't dance? Well I can prove them wrong.

SANDY dances, two Filipino girls wearing brown masks enter from side, pointing at SANDY.

GIRL 1:   Who the hell does she think she is?

GIRL 2:   Just walking in here, trying to be Wannabe Flip and all.

GIRL 1:   Great, now all of the quality guys are looking at her.

GIRL 2:   It's coz they think white girls are easy.

GIRL 1:   Why can't they go to their own rye bread and cheese socials?

GIRL 2:   Can't get her own colour, so she has to go all Asiaphile on us.

               Exits.

SANDY: Asiaphile—that's what they call me behind my back—because I've dated a few Asian guys. Okay, maybe more than a few: Three Filipinos, a Chinese guy, a Vietnamese guy and someone that's half-Japanese. I've dated white guys too, but it's the others that they care about. It's not like I hunt them out and rip them away from their Asian girlfriends. Although sometimes, it backfires and some guys assume I'm something else.

               SANDY continues dancing. Filipino guy wearing brown mask struts in, checking SANDY out. He tries to dance with her. She edges away. He has a thick, macho Filipino accent.

ASIAN GUY: Hey, what's your name?

SANDY: Sandy.

ASIAN GUY: You're hot.

SANDY: Uh, thanks, I guess.

ASIAN GUY: You wanna take a ride with me? My car is pretty sweet.

SANDY: Uh, I'm here with friends. And I don't even know you.

ASIAN GUY: My friends call me Sexy. You can call me that too.

SANDY: Sorry, I'm not interested.

ASIAN GUY: Come on. I know what you're here for.

SANDY: I'm here to have fun with my friends.

ASIAN GUY: It's just a little drive. I know what you girls are like. *(Grabs her wrist.)*

SANDY: Let go of me or I will break your hand.

              He pauses to assess her.

ASIAN GUY: White bitch. *(Walks away.)*

GIRL 1:   *(Entering from back.)* Did you see that? Now she thinks she's too good for our men. Why did she come here in the first place? *(Exits.)*

SANDY: I don't care what they say or what they think. I never did. I never will.

              Fade out.

Joke Lang (Just a Joke)

              Laugh track, spotlight on SIENNA as standup comedian.

SIENNA: What do you call a Filipino walking a dog? A vegetarian.

              Laugh track.

              What do you call a Filipino without a sewing machine? Unemployed.

Laugh track.

Why do Filipino guys have tiny mustaches? So they can look like their moms.

Laugh track.

Lights up.

MALAYA: Don't you care about being Filipino at all? *(Exits.)*

SANDY: You went too far, Sienna. *(Exits.)*

SIENNA: What? They're just jokes. They're funny. What?

Lights fade out.

Hero

Spotlight on SANDY.

SIENNA: Growing up, we all had heroes that we looked up to, a mold that we used to shape ourselves, the model we desperately tried to emulate. We were from a generation that had the television as a sitter and not a single brown girl in sight. There was plenty to choose from, depending on your tastes.

Lights up. The answers are childlike.

SANDY: My hero is Wonder Woman. She's just so cool! She's strong and she has a tiara and she has a lasso and she beats up on boys. She is like, so awesome!

SIENNA: I like *Charlie's Angels,* I don't have a favourite one yet, but I heard some of the boys talking about this picture of Farrah Fawcett in a red bathing suit. I think I want to be like that.

MALAYA: When I grow up, I want to be like Madonna, not the Virgin Mary Madonna, the blonde one, the one that sings and rolls around on the floor and shows off her belly button. She's pretty and very brave.

SIENNA: An Asian hero? Oh, I don't know. That's a little harder. Um, I guess Bruce Lee.

SANDY: I've heard of Bruce Lee. He kicks butt too.

MALAYA: There are lots of Filipino people I idolize. There's Sharon Cuenta and Donna Cruz and…

SIENNA: But they're all back in the Philippines.

SANDY: I've never heard of them.

SIENNA: I've seen pictures of them. They bleach their skin.

SANDY: Then they don't count. Pick someone else.

MALAYA: I don't know… Bruce Lee? *(Cross fade to spotlight.)*

SIENNA: We didn't have much to choose from back then. Chinese-American Bruce Lee was a household name, but he not only perpetuated the Asian Martial Arts stereotype, he created it.

             Lights fade up, first few bars of "Kung Fu Fighting" plays. 'Bruce' wearing brown mask and Ninja wearing brown mask bow towards each other then take sparring stance. When they speak, their lips continue to move, as in the era of dubbed martial arts movies.

             You killed my father!

SANDY: Ha ha! Yes, I used chopsticks and ninja stars.

SIENNA: You shall pay dearly for this.

             A pathetic fight scene ensues. SIENNA kicks in the air and SANDY is sent flying back.

             GIRL wearing brown mask throws her arms around Bruce.

GIRL: Bruce, you're my hero!

             Spotlight on MALAYA as she takes off the mask.

MALAYA: Then there's the hero that you have to find inside
               yourself, the one that you don't even realize is there
               until you need her.

                      Lights up.

SIENNA: One summer day when I was sixteen.

SANDY: I was fifteen.

MALAYA: I was sixteen.

SIENNA: Coming home from work.

SANDY: Coming home from the mall.

MALAYA: Coming home from the library.

                      *As they speak they set up the scene for the back seat of
                      a bus. A grey mask is set up on one of the seats.
                      SANDY, SIENNA and MALAYA take turns
                      playing the WOMAN by switching the grey mask
                      between them.*

SIENNA: It was raining.

SANDY: So I hopped on a downtown bus.

MALAYA: Heading for home.

SIENNA: I headed towards the back of the bus.

SANDY: There were two girls already there.

MALAYA: I had seen them around.

SIENNA: But I didn't really know them.

SANDY: I didn't mind though.

MALAYA: I just wanted to get home.

SIENNA: There were also two boys sitting near me.

SANDY: They were East Indian.

MALAYA: And a woman, maybe in her twenties.

SIENNA: It doesn't matter what race she was.

SANDY: At the next stop, the two boys stood up and ran out
               into the rain.

MALAYA: They looked so scared.

SIENNA: And the woman just laughed and laughed.

SANDY: Then the woman stood up.

MALAYA: And sat next to me.

SIENNA: I don't know why.

SANDY: There were plenty of other seats.

MALAYA: But she decided to sit next to me.

WOMAN: *(Played by SIENNA, talking to SANDY.)* These stupid
               Chinks. They keep stealing our jobs.

SANDY: Are you talking to me?

WOMAN: My man lost his job to one of them immigrants from
               China or Nam or wherever they're coming from.
               Now our kids gotta starve. It's like an invasion.
               They're taking over everything. You hear that,
               Chinky girl? You keep stealing our jobs, maybe I
               should steal the Toyota daddy got you.

MALAYA: I don't own a car.

WOMAN: You'll get a Honda and my tax money that went
               towards bringing your ass here will end up going to
               Japan.

SANDY: She isn't the cause of any of your problems.

WOMAN: Fucking Chink Lover. I bet you have a Chink
               boyfriend too.

SANDY: As a matter of fact, my boyfriend is Filipino.

WOMAN: Fucking Chink Wannabe.

MALAYA: We didn't do anything to you. Why are you picking on us?

WOMAN: Shut up, you slant-eyed Chinked up bitch.

> *SIENNA sits, MALAYA takes the place of the WOMAN.*

SIENNA: She's not even Chinese.

WOMAN: You have a problem with me too?

SIENNA: None of us have a problem with you.

WOMAN: All of you Chinks are my problem.

> *SANDY takes place of WOMAN.*

WOMAN: You think you can take me? Come on, Chink. Get up. I know kung-fu too.

> *Starts to feebly kick and punch at SIENNA and MALAYA, coming very close to their faces. They turn away. MALAYA takes place of WOMAN.*

SANDY: Just sit down.

WOMAN: Mind your own business or you're next. *(Close to SIENNA.)*

             You scared?

> *SIENNA tries to stand up, WOMAN pushes her back down to the seat.*

             Is that all you got? *(Laughs.)*

> *SANDY takes place of WOMAN.*

WOMAN: Come on, get up. Scared that you'll get some sweat on that mustache of yours?

MALAYA: Leave her alone!

WOMAN: Put your coolie back on and shut your trap!

SIENNA: Get out of my face.

WOMAN: Why don't you get your brown ass back to wherever
            it is you came from.

            You don't belong here. None of you belong here!

            Bus hits a bump, WOMAN stumbles and sits down.

MALAYA: Then the bus stops. The woman sat there,
            disoriented.

SANDY: We all stood up and ran out. Maybe not all of us.

SIENNA: *(Turning towards the back of the bus.)* I was born here,
            bitch. My brown ass is exactly where it belongs.
            Here. *(Runs off bus.)*

SANDY: We didn't run, even though it was raining.

MALAYA: We stood there watching as the bus drove away.

SIENNA: The woman in the back giving us the middle finger.

            *They give her the middle finger back, turning as it
            drives away. They turn to each other.*

            I'm Sienna.

SANDY: Sandy.

MALAYA: Malaya.

            They shake hands.

            Three spotlights.

SIENNA: I had never encountered racism before.

SANDY: I was one of those naive people who had forgotten
            that not everyone is colour blind.

MALAYA: How do I fight it? How do I fight them?

SIENNA: You don't.

SANDY: They say education is one way to fight.

MALAYA: Another is pride.

Lights up, they slowly walk towards each other.

SIENNA: Coconut.

MALAYA: Fob.

SANDY: Rice Lover.

SIENNA: Brown on the outside, white on the inside.

MALAYA: Fresh off the boat.

SANDY: Just love those Asian boys.

SIENNA: I finally belong somewhere.

MALAYA: With people who understand the need to fight.

SANDY: With people who understand the need for pride.

SIENNA: *I* belong here. *(Taking MALAYA's hand.)*

MALAYA: I *belong* here. *(Taking SANDY's hand.)*

SANDY: I belong *here.*

                Fade out.

                The End.

To Forgive, Divine

Joseph Aragon

Characters

JOYCE Valdes, 20

DOLORES Valdes, 50

Father NICK Domingo, 35

Time

Present

Place

Saint Ignatius Church; the Valdes' home; a prison

Prologue

Darkness. Silence.

A gunshot. Girl screaming. Another gunshot. People panicking, girl still screaming. Three more gunshots. The girl's screaming stops. Police scanner. Sirens. Police and paramedics scrambling. General street commotion. Vehicles peeling away, sirens blaring. Commotion continues, dies down.

Scene 1

Sound crossfades to a muffled piano playing a hymn in a different room.

Lights up on the sacristy of Saint Ignatius Church. JOYCE is folding some laundry. NICK enters.

JOYCE: So? How do you like the rectory?

NICK: I love it, I'll take it, where do I sign?

JOYCE: Father Stephen had eclectic taste in wall colours. You can paint over it if you want.

NICK: I don't mind it.

JOYCE: Okay then, I'll paint over it.

NICK: Not a big fan of taupe and purple?

JOYCE: Not a big fan of Father Stephen.

NICK: From what I've heard, the people here loved him.

JOYCE: Yes. They also love Lawrence Welk.

NICK: How do you think they'll react to me?

JOYCE: They'll hate you at first. Then, once they've gotten used to your style, they'll only mildly dislike you. Who knows, five years down the road you might win their complete indifference.

NICK: I like to aim high.

JOYCE: I think you can handle them. You're young and plucky enough.

NICK: When did you say your mom was coming?

JOYCE: She's probably on her way now. Went to buy some paper for the copier.

NICK: Dolores, right?

JOYCE: Yeah. She'll cover all the administration and finance stuff. Then she'll want to parade you in front of parish council, liturgy committee, maybe the CWL.

NICK: I'm looking forward to meeting her.

        JOYCE lets out a knowing chuckle.

        Well she sounded nice over the phone.

JOYCE: That's her secretary voice. You have to meet her in person for the full effect.

NICK: Sounds charming already.

        NICK watches JOYCE fold and put away more things.

        So! Tell me about yourself.

JOYCE: Excuse me?

NICK: Well—you've been showing me around the church, telling me things, being a gracious hostess, and I don't know a blessed thing about you.

JOYCE: You don't need to know anything about me.

NICK: Sure I do. You're the sacristan, we'll be seeing a lot of each other. *(Pause.)* Are you in school?

JOYCE: *(Still keeping busy.)* Yeah. U of M, second year. Psychology.

NICK: Impressive. Going into therapy, that kind of thing?

JOYCE: I just wanted to study something that interested me.

NICK: I took psych in my third year of seminary. A lot of dry theory.

JOYCE: I know.

NICK: It's good preparation for a lot of things, though. Counselling and stuff. I actually took it to prep for prison ministry.

JOYCE: *(Stops.)* Prison ministry.

NICK: Mm-hm. Did it for a while… The human mind is…pretty complex…

JOYCE: I'll bet.

NICK: Got any brothers or sisters?

JOYCE: I didn't show you the shed, did I?

NICK: What shed?

JOYCE: Right next to the garage there's a shed where we keep all the Nativity figures. We have a committee in charge of decorating the church throughout the year, and every Christmas they go all out with a display out front. It's really spectacular. They do a good job.

NICK: Something to look forward to. In nine months.

               A door is heard opening.

DOLORES: *(Off.)* Joyce!

JOYCE: There she is. Make a good first impression.

NICK: How does my collar look.

JOYCE: Roman.

              DOLORES enters with a box of copier paper.

DOLORES: Joyce, you left the rear door unlocked again.

JOYCE: Sorry, Mother.

DOLORES: Oh! Here's a new face.

NICK: But not a new voice, I hope.

DOLORES: We talked over the phone. *(Shakes his hand.)* Father Nicholas.

NICK: Dolores. Nice to finally meet you in person.

DOLORES: …You're rather young.

JOYCE: Mother…

NICK: If thirty-five is young, I'll take that as a compliment.

DOLORES: I'm sorry, Father Nicholas, I guess I got so used to Father Stephen.

NICK: Not a problem. And please—"Nick." You don't even have to call me Father, just "Nick."

DOLORES: Well—Father Nick—I'm glad you came when you did. We've had to share priests with other churches since Father Stephen retired. Did Joyce show you around?

JOYCE: Of course I did, Mother.

NICK: Gave me the grand tour and everything.

DOLORES: Good. *(Beat.)* I spoke to the pastor of Saint Jude's in Edmonton.

NICK: …Father Wilhelm. Yes.

DOLORES: He had many things to say about you.

NICK: Good things?

DOLORES: Things. Father Stephen was very popular around here. He was a charming, eloquent man. You have some very big shoes to fill.

NICK: And me a size seven. Don't worry, Dolores. I'll adapt.

DOLORES: Good.

NICK: Although... I would be remiss in my duties as a pastor if I didn't promote the spiritual growth of my congregation. And I personally believe that the best way to do that is to present fresh, exciting challenges to people. Challenges that engage the intellect and the soul. And I can tell already that you're the kind of person who would be up for that kind of thing.

DOLORES: Really. You think so.

NICK: Absolutely.

DOLORES: ...Well. We'll see, won't we.

NICK: Just as long as we both know we're on the same side.

DOLORES: It will be very interesting working with you.

NICK: With you too, Dolores. *(Realizes.)* Oh, damn, I almost forgot. Is that the lectionary?

JOYCE: Yeah.

NICK: *(Flipping through the pages.)* What is it, fourth Sunday of Lent? My first mass is tomorrow and I haven't written my homily yet. And I have to make it a good one, don't I? Let's see...Matthew five...Sermon on the Mount...okay. Well, I gotta get cracking. I shall now retire to my purple and taupe rectory and attempt to match Father Stephen's eloquence. It was really nice meeting you ladies.

DOLORES: Welcome to Saint Ignatius, Father Nick.

NICK: Good to be here. It's gonna be fun.

            NICK exits.

DOLORES: I hate him.

JOYCE: Mother!

DOLORES: Did you see that? We met only a moment ago and he's already antagonizing me!

JOYCE: What was all that about?

DOLORES: Did you see the smirk on his face? Cocky arrogance.

JOYCE: He's not cocky. A little goofy, maybe.

DOLORES: You left the door unlocked.

JOYCE: I'm sorry, Mother.

DOLORES: This is the third time I've told you this.

JOYCE: You're keeping count?

DOLORES: What time will you be home tonight?

JOYCE: I still have to clean out the font. I'll be home around six.

DOLORES: Good. We're going to the potluck at seven.

JOYCE: What? You never told me this.

DOLORES: Why. You don't have plans.

JOYCE: It doesn't matter if I have plans or not. You can't spring things on me at the last minute like this.

DOLORES: Do you have plans?

JOYCE: Well—yeah I do. Some friends and I were gonna go bowling.

DOLORES: Bowling.

JOYCE: Yeah. Glow bowling. At Academy. I'll be home by ten.

DOLORES: This is the parish council potluck. People will expect to see you there.

JOYCE: But I don't need to be there, do I?

DOLORES: No, but then I'd have to explain why you're not there.

JOYCE: Well then explain to them.

DOLORES: So you want me to say, "I'm sorry Joyce couldn't make it. She didn't think the parish council was important enough to have dinner with."

JOYCE: Mother, that's not fair.

DOLORES: Where are you really going tonight?

JOYCE: Bowling!

DOLORES: With friends.

JOYCE: Yes!

DOLORES: …You know what? Maybe I won't go to the potluck. Bowling sounds like fun. Maybe I'll come with you.

JOYCE: Mother!—

DOLORES: Sure, why not! I was quite the bowler in my day.

JOYCE: Stop it.

DOLORES: You are lying to me, Joyce.

JOYCE: Why would you say that!

DOLORES: Have you ever bowled a game in your entire life?

JOYCE: Of course I have!

DOLORES: You never told me you have.

JOYCE: There are a lot of things I never tell you.

DOLORES: I know.

JOYCE: ...What do you want, Mother. You want me to become a hermit? An old maid?

DOLORES: I want you to come to the dinner tonight.

JOYCE: Well I don't want to come to the dinner tonight.

DOLORES: Why not.

JOYCE: It's not exactly my crowd! I don't have a crowd at all thanks to you.

DOLORES: This dinner is important.

JOYCE: I don't give a shit about the dinner.

DOLORES: Language!

          NICK enters.

NICK: Is everything okay in here?

JOYCE: You can't keep me locked up! I'm twenty years old for Chrissake!—

DOLORES: I'm warning you—

NICK: —'cause really, I can help—

JOYCE: How many times do we have to have this same *fucking* argument!

DOLORES: Joyce!

          JOYCE storms off.

          I'm sorry you had to see that, Father.

          DOLORES goes after her daughter.

          NICK, seeing there's nothing to do, exits.

Scene 2

Sunday mass. NICK, in a purple vestment, is giving his first homily to his new congregation.

NICK: Okay. The way I understand how this works is that my job is to preach to you, and your job is to listen to me. So if you finish your job before I do, let me know.

Now, doubtless you've heard a few things about me already. I know what parish gossip is like. So I'm here to put your minds at ease and assure you that everything you've heard about me is absolutely true.

Don't worry. I won't thrust myself on you full-force just yet. We'll take baby steps. It's true that my methods are a bit unorthodox. But then, Jesus was a bit of an odd duck too, wasn't he. Hanging with lepers. Drinking with prostitutes. Picking grain from the field on the Sabbath—ooh, naughty. But he challenged the preconceptions of his day, while at the same time remaining a faithful and devoted Jew.

Which brings us to today's Gospel. The Sermon on the Mount. After all those "blessed are you"s and "you are the salt of the earth" he goes into a series of antitheses. "You have heard it said but I say to you…" "You have heard it said 'an eye for an eye,' but I say to you 'turn the other cheek'." "You have heard it said 'love your neighbour and hate your enemy,' but I say to you 'love your enemies and pray for those who persecute you'."

A noble philosophy. But who here actually does it? Who here actually takes Jesus at his word and *does* turn the other cheek? Who *does* love their enemies? Raise your hands. Anyone? Don't be shy . . .

I thought so. It's a hard teaching. It's counter-intuitive. It goes against common sense. But as

Christians, that's what we're called to do. To alter our perception. To think outside the box.

Here's an assignment for you. This week, I'd like you to perform a "Random Act of Kindness." You've heard of this before. Try just one random act. Pay for someone's meal at a restaurant. Plunk a loonie into someone's parking meter. Give flowers to a co-worker you never talk to. Doesn't matter if you know the person or even like the person. Do anything…as long as it doesn't make sense.

It's a nutty idea. But this really is the way you have to think. It may feel uncomfortable to you, but none of us became Christians to be comfortable… Right?

Scene 3

>   *The sacristy, after mass. NICK is putting away his vestment; JOYCE is rinsing and putting away chalices.*

JOYCE: That was a very cute homily.

NICK: Thank you.

JOYCE: How many people do you think will actually do it?

NICK: Precious few if any.

JOYCE: I've met my share of "wacky hip" priests, but I never thought one would become pastor of this parish.

NICK: Someone's gotta shake things up a little. When I entered the seminary, I promised myself never to turn into that jaded pampering priest who spits out token homilies. I would never bore my congregation into complacency.

JOYCE: Father Stephen beat you to it. It's no use trying to get a rise out of this crowd. If they had their way, we'd still be saying mass in Latin.

NICK: All the more reason to try. Call it young stupid idealism.

JOYCE: All right. It's young stupid idealism.

> *JOYCE keeps rinsing, wiping and putting things away. NICK watches with vexed interest for a long while until JOYCE feels his gaze on her. She finally turns to him.*

NICK: You're funny.

JOYCE: *(Beat.)* Thank you.

NICK: I mean—I'm getting this vibe from you. I get the feeling you're a much more interesting person than you let on.

JOYCE: …We're all interesting in our own little way. We all have talents and hobbies and stuff, little quirks.

You're an interesting person.

NICK: Am I.

JOYCE: Yeah, bounding into a parish like this, "shaking things up." It would be interesting to know what makes you tick, what brought you to this point. All the events in your life that…shape you…

> *Pause.*

NICK: Listen…I'm meeting with people at the care home at two o'clock. I heard you volunteer there.

JOYCE: Once in a while. Great bunch of people.

NICK: Yeah, so I was wondering—I don't know these people, you do, maybe you might wanna come with me, break the ice a bit. We could even grab lunch before we go if you want, shoot the breeze. Two interesting people like us should have lots to talk about.

JOYCE: …Well—Nick—I'd like to, but I have other stuff planned. Sorry.

NICK: …Oh well. Some other time, then.

JOYCE: Yeah, some other time, just not now…things are a little—weird.

NICK: …All right then. *(Pause; he consults his watch.)* I'll be in the rectory. *(NICK starts to leave.)*

JOYCE: I went to the potluck.

NICK: What?

JOYCE: The potluck. I ended up going to it.

NICK: Chalk one up for Mother.

JOYCE: Yeah. She can lay one hell of a guilt trip. That was not our finest hour yesterday.

NICK: Not a problem. Mother-daughter spats. It's normal.

JOYCE: A little too normal, for us.

NICK: Gosh, I hope your friends didn't miss you too much at the bowling lanes.

JOYCE: I wasn't going bowling.

NICK: I see. Who's the guy?

JOYCE: Someone my mother would definitely not approve of.

NICK: Why? Is he Satan?

JOYCE: No, just a nice, normal, sweet guy. Very un-Satan-like.

NICK: What's his name?

JOYCE: *(With meaning.)* Noah Weisenthal.

NICK: Oooh…

JOYCE: If she knew I was dating a Semite, she'd swallow her rosary.

NICK: I can see your dilemma. Is he cute at least?

JOYCE: He's okay. Nothing serious, though. He's just my excuse to get out of the house.

NICK: Why wasn't I invited to the potluck? This was parish council, right?

JOYCE: They were gossiping about you.

NICK: Ah.

JOYCE: You might as well have been the Antichrist, the way they were talking.

NICK: And so it continues.

JOYCE's cell phone rings.

JOYCE: (*Answers.*) Hello? ...Hey, you...

NICK: Speak of the devil!

JOYCE: Mm-hm? ...Yup, eight o'clock...'kay, see you tonight. Bye.

(*Hangs up; off NICK's look.*) I can't let her win, now, can I?

NICK: At least all this sneaking around adds intrigue to things.

JOYCE: Very Romeo and Juliet.

NICK: With a little Shylock thrown in. You think she'll find out about tonight?

JOYCE: Probably. I gotta hand it to her, she's got a keen mother's intuition. She was so sure I was lying yesterday. I'm a pretty good liar, but it was almost like she *knew*. Oh well, I'll do better tonight.

NICK: Here's hoping.

JOYCE: I'll see you tomorrow. Wish me luck.

NICK: Mazel tov.

             JOYCE exits.

Scene 4

             The Valdes home. DOLORES is seated, distraught.
             JOYCE enters.

JOYCE: Mother?

DOLORES: Oh. Hi.

JOYCE: I'm going to the library tonight to study. If that's
             okay with you.

DOLORES: It's late.

JOYCE: The university library. Extended hours.

DOLORES: Fine. Go. I'm in no mood to argue.

JOYCE: ...Is something wrong?

DOLORES: No. Nothing. I'm just tired.

JOYCE: *(Sees mail on the table.)* Any mail for me?

DOLORES: No.

             JOYCE sorts through the mail and spots an empty
             open envelope.

JOYCE: Corrections Canada?

DOLORES: It was nothing important.

JOYCE: It can't be about a parole hearing, that's four years
             away.

DOLORES: It was about nothing. Forget it.

JOYCE: Can I read it?

DOLORES: I threw it away.

JOYCE: Why?

DOLORES: It was nothing important!

JOYCE: Mother, this is addressed to both of us. You had no right to throw it away till I read it first. What was it about? Are they reopening Jim's case? Do we have to go to court? Does it have to do with Sawchuk? What?—

DOLORES: Joyce…please… You have to believe me. It was nothing. If it was important, of course I would have shared it with you. But it was nothing. Forget about it.

                I'm going to take a bath.

                DOLORES leaves.

                JOYCE rummages through the wastebasket under the table, but finds nothing. She leaves for the kitchen.

Scene 5

                NICK is in his office, working on another homily. JOYCE enters.

JOYCE: Hi, Nick. I need to talk to you.

NICK: Listen to this: A tourist wants to take a boat ride across the Sea of Galilee, asks the boatman "How much?" Boatman says "Fifty bucks." "Fifty bucks? No wonder Jesus walked!"

                Lead balloon pause.

JOYCE: I need to talk to you.

NICK: Sure. What about.

JOYCE: What do you know about this.

> *JOYCE gives him a crumpled pamphlet. NICK takes it, detects an odour, sniffs it.*

NICK: Mm. Interesting bouquet.

JOYCE: Meatloaf. Vintage last Tuesday.

NICK: "Project Lazarus— a new restorative justice initiative from the Correctional Service of Canada."

JOYCE: It's some weird kind of prison program. Rehabilitation of inmates. You said you did prison ministry, right?

NICK: We have a program like this in Alberta. Victim-offender mediation. Helps a lot of people.

JOYCE: How.

NICK: Face-to-face meetings, dialogue, dealing with emotions. It promotes healing.

JOYCE: Face-to-face?

NICK: Yeah. *(Beat.)* Would you mind my asking where you got this from?

JOYCE: …In the mail.

NICK: So you were involved in something…

> *Pause. JOYCE opens a filing cabinet and rifles through it. She pulls out a folder of newspaper clippings and hands it to NICK. He opens it.*

JOYCE: You were bound to find out sooner or later. Might as well hear it from me first.

NICK: "Student Killed in Attempted Robbery." *(Reads some more.)* You had a brother.

JOYCE: Jim. Yeah.

NICK: I'm sorry.

JOYCE: Why? You didn't shoot him. Don't even bother

reading the rest. It's boring. Some asshole bursts into a convenience store, shouts something about money, shots are fired, people start bleeding. Like a bad Crimestoppers video.

NICK: How many people were shot?

JOYCE: Just him and me.

NICK: ...You?

JOYCE: Yup. One in the chest, two in the right shoulder. *(Beat.)* How interesting am I now?

NICK: I'd say you're downright engrossing.

JOYCE: Well, there you have it. The enigma solved.

NICK: ...Wow ...This is... You'll have to forgive me, this is...wow.

JOYCE: Have I really changed that much in your eyes?

NICK: ...Yes. Is that wrong?

JOYCE: No. I should be used to it by now, I guess. I still can't get over how stupid the whole thing was. The guy who shot us—Michael Sawchuk of 812 Selkirk Avenue—what a fucking idiot! Can't hold up a fucking convenience store without spazzing out. Then there's the police, the doctors, the lawyers, especially that defense attorney, fuck I wanted to claw that bitch's eyes out—

             ...Sorry Nick.

NICK: Not a problem. You know what the shortest prayer in the world is?

JOYCE: What.

NICK: "Fuck it." It's a very honest prayer.

JOYCE: Fuck it. Fuck it, fuck it, fuck it, fuck it, fuck it! ...Sure beats a round of Hail Marys.

It was senseless, Nick. It didn't have to happen. He didn't have to shoot, I had the fucking till open, I was giving him the money! I dunno, something spooked him? —set him off somehow? I don't understand—

...this isn't healthy...this fucking pamphlet!—...You know what, forget it. Mother was right, just—forget it.

JOYCE takes the pamphlet, crumples it.

NICK: Wait. Lemme ask you something. How have things been since then. This was—two years ago, it looks like?

JOYCE: Yeah. My therapist said the first year is the hardest, when you hit all the holidays and anniversaries. This year was a little easier, with the trial out of the way.

NICK: So you and your mother are coping well?

JOYCE: You saw yourself how "well" we're coping. We try to avoid each other when we can, which, unfortunately, isn't often, thank you Saint Ignatius. Mother buries herself in her work. Spends a lot of time with her potluck pals from parish council. And me, I've got school. And I've got Dreidel Boy. That's my pet name for him now.

NICK: That's precious.

JOYCE: It's not the healthiest way of coping, but there it is.

NICK: Did you have nightmares, mood swings, things like that?

JOYCE: ...I used to cry a lot. Uncontrollable sobbing fits, they hit without warning, not much anymore though... Nightmares. Still have 'em... And I jump at sudden loud noises. A balloon pops, a car backfires—ridiculous how many times I've freaked out. It's Pavlovian.

And I've become slightly agoraphobic. Jim and I used to take walks outside, talk about stuff. Gorgeous spring day, blue sky, I used to love it. Now I can't go anywhere without looking over my shoulder. I turn wide when I walk around corners. And as for the outdoorsy beauty-of-Nature thing… I can't see it anymore. The world has become a very ugly place for me. So many horrible things happen in it.

Yeah, I know. I never used to be this cynical. I was a happy girl. I was cheerful and sweet and blissfully ignorant.

It's been two years. How come I'm not feeling at least a little better? I went to a fucking shrink! I even tried praying, a little. Things just— *(Trails off.)*

NICK: *(Taking the pamphlet.)* Is that why you came to me with this?

JOYCE: …I just wanted to know if you knew anything about it. Not like I was actually gonna—you know…

NICK: Why not?

JOYCE: Well—c'mon, Nick… It's nuts! The last thing I want to do is meet this guy face-to-face—I mean—what do I have to say to him?

NICK: Starting a dialogue can be a healthy thing, you deal with unresolved issues—

JOYCE: What's unresolved? He killed Jim, he got convicted, he went to jail, case closed. Literally. Neat and tidy.

NICK: It's never that simple, Joyce.

JOYCE: What, you're gonna tell me he's really a nice guy who fell in with the wrong crowd?

NICK: Well what was his upbringing like?

JOYCE: Broken home, dad was a drunk, all that shit. God knows the defense was trying to play it up. And I know where you're going with that and I don't buy it. Not everyone who comes from a broken home turns into a murderer.

NICK: Yeah but the environment doesn't exactly promote an alternate career choice.

JOYCE: Why the hell are you defending him?

NICK: I'm not defending him. I'm just trying to get a balanced view here.

JOYCE: Is my view that skewed? Am I really that blind to reason?

NICK: No. But you're definitely not impartial.

JOYCE: …You know what? Fuck it. Forget I even brought it up.

NICK: Joyce—

JOYCE: Forget it! I'm not gonna listen to you make excuses for him! Michael Sawchuk is an evil murderous prick and that's that!

NICK: Joyce listen! …Okay, fine, I'm clueless, all right? I don't know what it's like to have three bullets rip through me and God willing I never will. But I do know that you have an opportunity here. For healing. You said yourself you weren't getting any better. This could be just the thing to get you in the right direction.

JOYCE: How!

NICK: By sharing your stories. By telling yours and listening to his.

JOYCE: And why should I give a fuck about his story!

NICK: Because he has a right to tell it.

Pause.

JOYCE: What?

NICK: He has a right to tell his story. He has a right to be
            heard.

JOYCE: And what about Jim. He had some rights too.

NICK: Joyce—

JOYCE: Fuck you, Nick.

            JOYCE exits. NICK is alone.

Scene 6

            *The Valdes home. JOYCE enters with her backpack,
            flops into a chair. DOLORES enters.*

DOLORES: Where were you.

JOYCE: I was studying.

DOLORES: No you weren't.

JOYCE: I was at the church.

DOLORES: Doing what.

JOYCE: Sacristan stuff.

DOLORES: It's not your day.

JOYCE: That's an understatement.

DOLORES: What were you doing there.

JOYCE: What, I can't pick up a few extra hours at the church
            if I feel like it?

DOLORES: You could. But you didn't.

JOYCE: I am not in the mood for this.

            DOLORES grabs JOYCE's backpack and opens it.

            Mother—!

DOLORES pulls out the pamphlet.

DOLORES: I can't believe you went into the garbage to get this. I threw spoiled meatloaf on it. *(Rips it up.)* I don't want you doing this.

JOYCE: I wasn't going to.

DOLORES: Then why did you bother digging this up?

JOYCE: I wanted to know what it was about! I don't appreciate having my mail thrown out before I read it.

DOLORES: Did you read it?

JOYCE: Yes.

DOLORES: And?

JOYCE: I thought it was bullshit.

DOLORES: There you are, then. We both reached the same conclusion. If you listened to me in the first place, you'd have saved yourself a trip to the garbage.

JOYCE: It's the principle, Mother— ...Never mind. Forget it. Let's just forget it and life can get back to normal. Whatever the hell that is.

DOLORES: Where's that attitude coming from? You were such a nice girl.

JOYCE: I'm going up to my room to study.

DOLORES: So what did Father Nick have to say about it?

JOYCE: What makes you think I talked to Father Nick?

DOLORES: Well you certainly didn't go to church to pray.

JOYCE: He thought it was a good idea.

DOLORES: I swear, that man.

JOYCE: It promotes healing, he said.

DOLORES: I can tell the congregation is none too thrilled with him. And I've already phoned the Archbishop.

JOYCE: You're just not used to him yet.

DOLORES: It's a priest's responsibility to sustain the parish community with his leadership. And I don't see how he can do that if he alienates everyone with his stand-up comedy routine. And now he's messing with our personal lives.

JOYCE: Well we're stuck with him for a couple of years at least. Priests are scarce.

DOLORES: I don't want you spending any more time at the church than you need to. Keep your conversations with Father Nick to a minimum.

JOYCE: Aren't you overreacting?

DOLORES: I mean it, Joyce. I truly dislike the man.

JOYCE: Sure, Mother. Whatever you say.

DOLORES: I also dislike that tone in your voice.

JOYCE: Please! Gimme room to breathe, I'm tired, I'm pissed off— …*(Calmer.)* Yes, Mother, whatever you say. I won't talk to Father Nick unless I absolutely have to. Was that tone better?

            Screw studying, I'm just gonna go to bed.

DOLORES: Are you doing anything on Saturday?

JOYCE: Why.

DOLORES: Are you doing anything on Saturday.

JOYCE: …I'm meeting with my project group that evening.

DOLORES: Really.

JOYCE: Yes, really. Why.

DOLORES: You know that Jim's anniversary is coming up.

JOYCE:	Yeah, in about three weeks.
DOLORES:	I scheduled a prayer meeting for him at eight o'clock this Saturday.
JOYCE:	What?
DOLORES:	And you can't say I sprung this on you. I've given you ample warning and I expect you to be there.
JOYCE:	Why didn't you schedule it on the actual date?
DOLORES:	Because it'll be near Holy Week and everyone will be busy.
JOYCE:	Well—I know it's for Jim and all but—school's important. It's a group project.
DOLORES:	You're going to choose a group project over the memory of your brother?
JOYCE:	God, Mother, don't put it like that!
DOLORES:	This is far more important than any "group project", Joyce!
JOYCE:	A prayer meeting's no big deal, why can't we just reschedule, we've got time.
DOLORES:	I set it for Saturday.
JOYCE:	But Saturday's not convenient for me.
DOLORES:	Neither was Jim's death, was it.
JOYCE:	Jesus Christ!—
	DOLORES glares at her.
	Sorry—Mother—
DOLORES:	I'm concerned about you, Joyce. You don't go to prayer meetings, your attitude is embarrassing, and every second word out of your mouth is a blasphemy.

JOYCE: Look I just—I don't like going to those prayer meetings, okay? They're just— ...I don't see the point.

DOLORES: You're praying for your brother's soul.

JOYCE: I know but—he was a good guy, he probably made it to Heaven. He doesn't need any more help, does he?

DOLORES: You're making light of this.

JOYCE: ...I know. I don't mean to.

DOLORES: Please, Joyce. Do this for my sake. I know you don't take these things seriously anymore but I do.

JOYCE: I do too, Mother.

DOLORES: You don't.

JOYCE: ...It's not that I don't want to, I just ...can't.

DOLORES: *(After some thought.)* I remember, at Jim's funeral, Mrs. d'Angelo coming to console me, and she said the most beautiful thing to me. She compared God's creation to a tapestry. When you look at it from the back, it's all mess and tangles. Threads going all over the place. Tied in knots. Cut short. But it has to be that way because that's what creates the beautiful pattern in the front. Does that make sense to you?

JOYCE: ...a little...

DOLORES: Things make sense when you have faith, Joyce. God is gracious and good and whatever happens to us, good or bad, happens for a reason. We may not know that reason, but God does. And we have to trust that His reasons are for a greater good.

              No matter how we feel.

              Come to the meeting. Try your best to participate. Please do this for me. Do this for Jim.

JOYCE: ...okay.

DOLORES: Thank you.

                *DOLORES kisses JOYCE and exits. JOYCE is
                alone.*

Scene 7

                *NICK's office, the next day. NICK is consulting a
                lectionary and writing notes.*

                JOYCE knocks and enters. An awkward moment.

JOYCE: ...Hi.

NICK: ...Hi.

JOYCE: ...What are you up to.

NICK: Planning out my homilies for the next month. I
                usually start off with a joke, but I can't think of any
                good ones.

JOYCE: ...There's this Vicar. And he's doing confessions
                'cause the Pastor's away on vacation, but the Pastor
                left him this list of which penance to give for which
                sin, like "swearing equals one Hail Mary" and so on.
                So a woman comes into the booth and says "Bless
                me Father for I have sinned, I gave my boss a
                blowjob." So he searches the list for "blowjob", can't
                find it. Just then, Timmy the altar boy passes by and
                the Vicar asks him, "Quick, what does the Pastor
                give for a blowjob?" Timmy says, "A can of Coke
                and a bag of chips."

                Pause.

NICK: I'm thinking no.

JOYCE: No? I think it'll go over gangbusters with the
                congregation.

NICK: I'll run it by the liturgy committee.

Pause.

...I'm sorry.

JOYCE: You were only trying to help.

NICK: Some help I was. That's one thing I haven't mastered yet. Tact. *(Closes the book.)* So. Other than insulting my profession, any other reason for this visit?

JOYCE: Spite.

NICK: That's always a good reason.

JOYCE: My mother forbade me to talk to you. She thinks you're corrupting me.

NICK: I think you're doing a good enough job on your own.

JOYCE: *(Beat.)* Yesterday was the first time, in a very long time, that I talked about the shooting with anyone. There's an unspoken agreement around here never to talk about it.

NICK: That's never healthy.

JOYCE: I know. *(Beat.)* I never knew I was that angry. That I was *still* that angry. You talked about unresolved issues. I think I know what you mean now. So many questions.

NICK: Like?

JOYCE: ..."Why?" Why did you shoot? Why did you need a gun? Why did you have to rob a store? Why can't you get a fucking job and make money the way you're supposed to? And yeah, I know Sawchuk had a shitty life, fell in with the wrong crowd, but that is no excuse! Think about it, what kind of person would point—not even fire but just *point*—a real, loaded pistol at someone. And the power that person has—and he had to be aware of it—the power he has to actually destroy a human life, what kind of person would—*revel* in that kind of power, get his rocks off on it. And how evil does a person have to be to point a gun at a living human being and *deliberately* pull the trigger. I don't care how shitty your life was, you had to override a *lot* of basic human decency to get to that point. This was a deliberate, conscious, evil act.

How can you tell I've been thinking about this a lot.

I want to get into his head. Partly out of curiosity, but mostly— ...I just want to understand why.

NICK: And you're starting to think this program can help.

JOYCE: I don't know. *(Pause.)* Convince me.

NICK: What?

JOYCE: My mind is as open as it's ever gonna be right now, so this is your window of opportunity. Sell me on it. Why should I do this.

NICK: *(Beat.)* ...okay...all right...well, you said you had questions. This can go a long way toward answering those questions.

JOYCE: All right, go on.

NICK: And...with those answers will come understanding, and with that comes healing. For both you and him.

JOYCE: For him.

NICK: Yes.

JOYCE: And why should I care about him. This is where you lost me last time, so be careful.

NICK: ...What was Sawchuk charged with?

JOYCE: Manslaughter.

NICK: When's he up for parole?

JOYCE: In four years.

NICK: So in four years, potentially, he's free. He's out in civilized society, angry that years of his life were wasted in jail. He's pissed off at the world, nothing essentially has changed for him, so he pulls another crime. That's one scenario.

Another scenario: He did his time, he learned his lesson and he wants to set himself straight. But when he moves into a new neighbourhood and people learn that he killed someone, he's treated like a leper. And when people think you're a criminal asshole, you're eventually going to become a criminal asshole. So he re-offends.

Now. If someone were to intervene in all of this, if someone were to take the time to listen to him, to offer him guidance, to be his ally and advocate as he makes the transition back into society, then the chances of him pulling the same shit all over again are greatly reduced.

So that, in a nutshell, is why you should care.

JOYCE: …So what's in it for me.

NICK: What do you mean.

JOYCE: He's the one getting all the perks out of this deal. What do I get? A warm fuzzy? "I nursed him back to health and I set him free!" He's a murderer, not a raccoon.

NICK: …True, not much is in it for you, nothing tangible anyway. Except maybe a sense of closure. And satisfaction. After the trial was over, were you satisfied that justice had been served?

JOYCE: …No.

NICK: You weren't. And that's usually the case. 'Cause you didn't get to tell your side of the story. Other than your testimony, you probably didn't have much input. You didn't have a voice. But now, you do.

JOYCE: Too little too late the way I see it.

NICK: But it's something. *(Beat.)* The damage has been done. It can't be fixed. And unless Sawchuk can travel back in time and un-shoot your brother, no solution will be completely satisfying. So the best we can do is salvage what's left and try to make something good come out of it.

Pause.

JOYCE: I'm sorry, Nick. I *guess* you make sense but—talking with this guy—face-to-face, on even terms—it's—

NICK: Counter-intuitive?

JOYCE: …Paying for a stranger's meal is one thing, but this? I know what you're saying, forgiveness and mercy and shit like that, but you're asking a lot.

NICK: Yeah, it is asking a lot. It means thinking differently and examining new ways of looking at justice.

JOYCE: When I think of justice, I think of fairness. I think of a balancing of the scales. And you're asking me to tip those scales, and not in my favour.

Pause. NICK gathers his thoughts.

NICK: Back in seminary, I wrote a sermon for homiletics class. "The Problem of Fear," I called it. It had a brilliant beginning. "What is the opposite of love? The opposite of love is not hate. The opposite of love is not indifference. The opposite of love…is *fear*." Then I go on, with much style and flair, to explain how fear is the root cause of evil, the main obstacle to peace. Wars—fear of the "other", fear of the enemy. Street violence, gangs—fear of not belonging, fear of being inferior or powerless. Any evil act, from drive-by shootings to the Holocaust, is motivated by fear. But it's not just the acts themselves. The *responses* to those acts are also motivated by fear.

JOYCE: And what, do you think, are my fears.

NICK: ...The fear of losing control? ...fear of being vulnerable? ...fear of tipping the scales?...

JOYCE: *(Beat.)* ...so...how did you end this sermon of yours.

NICK: I quoted Paul. "Since fear has to do with..." Shit, how'd it go, wait a sec—

> *He grabs a Bible from his desk and flips through it, finds the passage:*

"Since fear has to do with punishment, love is not perfect in one who is afraid. There is no fear in love. Perfect love casts out fear."

JOYCE: Gosh, that's pretty.

NICK: I thought so.

JOYCE: So you want me to do the Good Christian Thing and "love" Michael Sawchuk.

NICK: It really is thinking differently, Joyce. It's thinking like a saint.

JOYCE: ...I can't. Bottom line, Nick, I'm not Jesus. I'm not the Virgin Mary or Saint Francis or Mother Teresa. I'm a regular, unsaintly human. I get scared. I get angry. I hate. And you would be the same way. You're no better than I am.

NICK: I didn't say I was.

JOYCE: It is so easy for you to say this shit, I mean *you've* never— *(Beat.)* Do *you* have any brothers or sisters?

NICK: ...Terry. She's thirty.

JOYCE: Well let's say Terry's shopping in a convenience store, some prick with a pistol bursts in and shoots up the place and she ends up in a body bag. When the police come knocking at your door at three in the morning, how do you think you're gonna feel.

NICK: …shocked…angry—

JOYCE: Pretty *fucking* shocked and angry.

NICK: I know I'm never gonna fully understand—

JOYCE: That's right. You're not. Unless you go through it yourself, you know absolute shit!—

NICK: But I know people who *have* gone through it—

JOYCE: Oh fuck that!

NICK: Joyce listen—

JOYCE: No! …No. *(Pause, breathes.)* Okay, look, this isn't constructive. I don't want to get angry at you again so let's step back from it for now.

NICK: …Okay.

JOYCE: We'll talk later. "Round Two."

NICK: Sure.

JOYCE: *(Beat.)* The more I talk about it, the more I think it's a bad idea. It doesn't feel right, and honestly, I think it'll do more harm than good.

I know Mother and I aren't in the best shape right now. But that could change. It's been two years, but who's to say two years is enough? It'll take a long time, I know it will, but we'll get better.

I should let you get back to—

NICK: Yeah.

JOYCE: …We will get better.

JOYCE goes to leave. NICK, in frustration, throws his Bible onto the desk with a sharp bang. JOYCE screams hysterically. NICK is startled. They look at each other.

Scene 8

Office reception desk. DOLORES is on the phone with the Archbishop.

DOLORES: But surely you've been getting other complaints... Yes, Your Grace, I know, but you have to understand, there's an environment here that demands a certain style of leadership, and I'm not convinced that Father Nick is up to the task. Can't we switch with Saint Anthony's? Father Pierre's a wonderful priest, even if he is French... Yes, I realize, but at the same time, a shortage doesn't necessarily entail a dearth of good pastoral leadership... No, Your Grace, I'm implying no such thing. I respect your judgment. The last thing I want is to be rude or disrespectful to you—

NICK enters.

NICK: Hey, Dolores.

DOLORES quickly hangs up on the Archbishop.

Hope that wasn't anyone important.

DOLORES: You startled me.

NICK: I didn't mean to.

The phone rings.

You better answer that. The Archbishop is a busy man.

DOLORES answers the phone.

DOLORES: Saint Ignatius Church, Dolores speaking ...I'm

sorry, Your Grace, we were unexpectedly cut off. Can I call you sometime tomorrow to…discuss the matter more? …Thank you …You have a good day too. Goodbye.

(Hangs up.) …How was your trip to the care home.

NICK: Good. Depressing, but good. Any messages for me?

DOLORES: No.

NICK: Any messages *about* me?

DOLORES: …Not today.

NICK: I'll be in my office.

DOLORES: Father …Can we talk?

NICK: Sure. That's why they pay me the big bucks. What's on your mind.

DOLORES: …This parish is going through a transitional phase. It's an awkward time for everyone involved, including yourself, I'm sure. And the congregation—I don't know if you've noticed, but they're a little slow warming up to a new personality.

NICK: You don't say.

DOLORES: So…I think that someone should take the initiative…to make the process a little less…painful.

NICK: My style is my style, Dolores. You can't expect me to be Father Stephen.

DOLORES: I expect nothing of the sort. And I can appreciate the importance of preserving one's "style". You're "hip", you're "with it" and I'm…"cool" with that. But you have to consider your target audience, Father. Have you taken a good look at who's in those pews?

NICK: I can understand your concern. And maybe I have been coming on too strong and I'm trying to scale back. But this is who I am. This is the reason I became a priest. I'm just acting on principle. And he's a rotten priest who doesn't live by principle.

It's four-thirty. You should go home.

DOLORES: I wish you'd alter your approach a little.

NICK: *(Walking toward his office.)* Go home. Read a good book.

DOLORES: I just don't want a repeat of Saint Jude!

NICK stops.

NICK: ...Just out of curiosity... What did Father Wilhelm tell you about my time at Saint Jude. *(Pause.)* He probably said some unkind words. Don't be afraid to repeat them.

DOLORES: ...Well...he said...and I'm paraphrasing heavily ...that—you are a crass, careless, foolish priest who doesn't know his limits.

NICK: ...And that's paraphrasing, you say.

DOLORES: Yes.

NICK: Is that all he told you?

DOLORES: Is there more?

NICK: ...No. I guess not. Not as far as Saint Jude is concerned. *(Pause.)* Go home, Dolores.

DOLORES: There's something you're not telling me.

NICK: Go home.

DOLORES: Why won't you tell me? It can't be that bad, unless you...Oh my God, you didn't—you're not a—Oh my God!—

NICK:	No, Dolores, it's not like that!—
DOLORES:	Oh my God!
NICK:	Relax! Calm down! It's not that! It's not that.
DOLORES:	It's not?
NICK:	No, of course not.
DOLORES:	Are you sure?
NICK:	I wouldn't be here if it were. Now go home.
DOLORES:	Then what is it? Why won't you tell me?
NICK:	...It's something that you don't need to hear right now. Trust me.
DOLORES:	...All right. I'm used to being kept in the dark. When you're ready to tell me, you'll tell me.
	(Beat.) I think I'll go home.
NICK:	Splendid idea.
DOLORES:	I'll see you tomorrow, Father.
	DOLORES starts to leave just as JOYCE enters.
JOYCE:	Oh! Mother. You're here late.
DOLORES:	No, you're here a half hour early.
JOYCE:	...I just want to get a head start on things.
DOLORES:	Really. *(To NICK.)* Has Joyce been doing a good job around here, Father?
NICK:	Yes. Very efficient. Sometimes I'm locked in my office, I hardly even know she's there. I come out and it's like the Cleaning Fairy came by for a visit.
DOLORES:	I'm glad to hear it.
	(To JOYCE.) I'll see you tonight.

JOYCE: I'll be home by seven.

DOLORES: You'll be home by six-thirty.

JOYCE: Yes, Mother.

              DOLORES leaves.

              "Cleaning Fairy?"

NICK: Either that or "Pixie".

JOYCE: I want you to read something.

              JOYCE hands NICK a letter. NICK scans it.

NICK: Oh, my.

JOYCE: I just found myself writing it. I wanted to try it out.
              The pamphlet said that it usually starts with written
              correspondence, so…

NICK: I thought your mom ripped it up.

JOYCE: I got another one.

NICK: Does this mean you'll do it?

JOYCE: It means I'm thinking about it.

NICK: Well …good, I'm glad you're at least thinking about
              it.

JOYCE: And it's going to take some preparation too, right?

NICK: Right.

JOYCE: If I go ahead with this, I need you to help me.

NICK: Sure, I can contact Corrections for you, hook you up
              with a mediator.

JOYCE: Actually, I want you to help me personally.

              (Beat.) I trust you.

NICK: You'd be better off with someone else.

JOYCE: Why? You did prison ministry, right? You have the background for this kind of thing.

NICK: But I'm new here. You'd probably have to deal with someone more familiar with the local system. I'll help you as much as I can, but I shouldn't be officially involved—

JOYCE: Please, Nick, I need someone I trust to help me through this and I don't want it to be some government employee.

NICK: …I'll see what I can arrange.

JOYCE: Thank you. One more thing.

NICK: What.

JOYCE: If I do this…Mother can't know.

NICK: …Hm. Tricky.

JOYCE: I thought, with the correspondence thing, I can use Noah's mailing address.

NICK: Dreidel Boy?

JOYCE: Yeah, Dreidel Boy. I can't use our home address or the church's. Mother'll see it for sure. Noah will call me if there's a response.

NICK: …I dunno, all this sneaking around…

JOYCE: She's dead set against it, Nick. If she finds out about this, heads will roll. And not just mine.

NICK: …Fine. Mother is out of the loop.

JOYCE: Thank you.

NICK: *(Beat.)* So? How did it feel. Writing that letter.

JOYCE: Weird. It's pretty stand-offish, isn't it.

NICK: Understandable.

JOYCE: This is crazy. Giving him a second chance like this.

NICK: That's what it's all about. *Redemption*. That's the entire witness of the Christian faith.

JOYCE: …You've really bought into the whole thing, haven't you.

NICK: If you don't buy it, you can't sell it.

JOYCE: So sure. No room for doubt.

NICK: …Well, I wouldn't say that. There's always room for a little doubt.

JOYCE: Are you telling me that the great Father Nicholas Domingo actually doubts?

NICK: …Well—

JOYCE: Oh my God, my hero has feet of clay!—

NICK: All I'm saying is that with any healthy faith, there's always room for doubt. Doubting leads to questions, questions lead to answers, and answers lead to a stronger faith.

JOYCE: Or more questions.

NICK: …Yeah. That too.

JOYCE: And where did your doubting lead you?

NICK: *(Beat.)* It led me here.

JOYCE: So, you're not as naive an idealist as I thought you were. You get more and more interesting every day.

           JOYCE's cell phone rings.

           (Answers.) Hello? …Hey, you.

NICK: *(Sings.)* "Dreidel, Dreidel, Dreidel, I made it out of clay…"

JOYCE: Oh be quiet.

NICK: I'll leave you two alone.

JOYCE: I still wanna talk some more about the details.

NICK: I'll be in my office.

            NICK goes into his office.

JOYCE: *(Into cell.)* Sorry about that...I'm good... Listen, good thing you called. We have to cancel Saturday...I know, me too, but I have to go to a prayer meeting...

Scene 9

            The Valdes home. DOLORES is reading a magazine. JOYCE enters, drops her purse on a table.

DOLORES: Hi.

JOYCE: Hey.

DOLORES: How was school.

JOYCE: Good.

DOLORES: Going anywhere this evening?

JOYCE: No. I'm gonna be a nun.

DOLORES: Glad to hear it.

JOYCE: I'm going to take a shower.

DOLORES: Mm-hm.

            Pause.

JOYCE: How was *your* day.

DOLORES: ...fine, I guess...worked at the church...we got a few new cases of wine.

JOYCE: White this time?

DOLORES: Yes. People were complaining about the red. It does little good to receive the Blood of Christ when you're gagging on it.

JOYCE: …Well…good…anything else?

DOLORES: …No.

JOYCE: I'm going to take a shower.

DOLORES: Mm.

> *Pause. JOYCE exits.*
>
> *DOLORES keeps pretending to read her magazine. Joyce's cell phone rings within her purse. She lets it ring until it stops. Making sure the coast is clear, DOLORES takes the cell from JOYCE's purse. She presses a series of buttons to access Joyce's voice mail. She listens to a message.*
>
> *JOYCE enters.*

JOYCE: What the hell are you doing with my cell phone.

> *Pause.*

DOLORES: Why are you doing this, Joyce—

JOYCE: No, no, what are you doing with my cell phone!—

DOLORES: Don't use that tone with me—

JOYCE: You're breaking into my voice mail! I can use any tone I fucking well want!

DOLORES: Joyce!

JOYCE: How long have you known my password. Have you been spying on me ever since I got the thing?

DOLORES: You're avoiding the issue.

JOYCE: *You're* avoiding the issue!

DOLORES: Why are you writing letters to that man!

JOYCE: It's none of your business. Nothing is your business!

DOLORES: This *is* my business, Joyce—

JOYCE: You broke into my voice mail! What kind of mother does that!

DOLORES: A mother who doesn't trust her daughter and rightfully so. You've been lying to my face for the past month. Where you're going, what you're doing, who you're with.

JOYCE: And you've been lying too. Pretending you didn't know anything.

DOLORES: Well I couldn't let on that I knew your password, could I?

JOYCE: Goddamnit, Mother!

DOLORES: Why are you writing to him!

JOYCE: It's none of your business!

DOLORES: This man killed your brother, Joyce. This man killed my son.

JOYCE: I know this.

DOLORES: Then why!

JOYCE: I don't know.

DOLORES: That's a fine answer. You don't know. Little Miss Logical and Rational, who thinks before she acts, doesn't know why she put pen to paper to write her brother's killer a letter.

JOYCE: It seemed like the right thing to do.

DOLORES: And who, pray tell, told you that. *(Pause.)* Don't listen to Father Nick. He's running our church into the ground.

JOYCE: He's only been here a month!—

DOLORES: And look what he's got you doing. He's confused you.

JOYCE: I am not confused. I did write that letter for a purpose.

DOLORES: What purpose!

JOYCE: I want to see if it helps!

DOLORES: ...Is it really all that bad? Are we really coping all that poorly?

JOYCE: Yes we are.

DOLORES: I don't believe that.

JOYCE: Fine. Don't. Believe what you want, don't believe what you want, as always. I just wish I had your gift for self-delusion.

DOLORES: And what is that supposed to mean.

JOYCE: Mother, we are not at a well place. We're constantly at each other's throats.

DOLORES: That's because you insist on lying to me at every turn.

JOYCE: And why do you think I lie? Ever since Jim died you've been keeping tabs on me.

DOLORES: You can't blame a mother for caring about her daughter.

JOYCE: I can blame you for smothering me. What, you're afraid I'm gonna get shot again? I think I've fulfilled my bullet quota for the next ten years.

DOLORES: I *am* afraid. Forgive me for being illogical and emotional but yes I am afraid.

JOYCE: You've got to let me get on with my life! I've got to see people again. I've got to connect with people.

DOLORES: Like Noah Weisenthal?

JOYCE: …Noah listens to me. I can tell him anything.

DOLORES: So you'll tell the truth to the likes of him but you'll lie to me.

JOYCE: You know why I go out with him? Because he's everything you're not. He's sensitive, he's Jewish, and he's *sane*! Every date with him is a vacation from you, and I savour every single one. Or I used to, before all your potlucks and prayer meetings got in the way— *(Suddenly realizes.)* …oh my God!

DOLORES: Joyce—

JOYCE: Oh my GOD!! How could you!

DOLORES: Joyce, listen to me—

JOYCE: I know you never liked my taste in guys but COME ON!!

DOLORES: Please, let me explain!—

JOYCE: What is there to explain! You broke into my voice mail, you knew when I was going out with Noah— *Christ!* To think that was all *deliberate*!? The potluck, the prayer meeting—Jesus, Mother, the prayer meeting, you used *Jim's prayer meeting* to stop me from seeing Noah!? What the *hell* was going through your mind! I sat through that meeting for *Jim*! Because I wanted to remember *Jim*! 'Cause I thought it was all about *Jim*!—

DOLORES: It was for Jim—

JOYCE: But you—Oh my God, Mother, this is sick, how could you do this!—

DOLORES: Please Joyce—

JOYCE: *Why* would you do this! You exploited his memory for such a petty reason—Why!

DOLORES: *Because I don't want Jewish grandchildren!*

Silence.

JOYCE: …oh this is so fucked up…

DOLORES: I don't. I just don't!

JOYCE: — this is so fucked up—

DOLORES: If Jim were alive, maybe it would be different. Jim had plans. Jim had Rachel. You remember Rachel.

JOYCE: She wasn't Catholic.

DOLORES: But she wasn't Jewish.

JOYCE: Oh my God, this isn't healthy, can't you see that what you're doing isn't healthy!

DOLORES: And what you're doing is?

JOYCE: It could lead to something.

DOLORES: To what? What good could it possibly do to sit in the same room with that man and watch him smirk at you. Like he did at the trial. You think you're up for that? You think a man like that can ever be sorry for what he's done?

JOYCE: I need to find that out for myself.

DOLORES: Why? Why can't you just let him rot in jail?

JOYCE: Because I have to do *something*! Because anything is better than this! Especially better than what *you're* doing! Your work, your parish council, your potlucks—

DOLORES: It's a source of strength, Joyce. Something you can't understand.

JOYCE: What good has it done you. What good have all those prayer meetings and novenas and Hail Marys and fellowships done. You're still bitter, you're still afraid, you're still angry, it's all *still there*. It's denial, Mother.

DOLORES: I have nothing to be in denial about. Of course I'm afraid. Of course I'm angry. I've always been honest about my feelings. I have nothing to hide.

JOYCE: Yes you do. *(Beat.)* You're angry at God.

DOLORES: …I am not.

JOYCE: I remember them all at Jim's funeral. "Oh, Jim's in heaven now, he's probably looking down on you right now" or "God must be testing you, he's testing your strength." Did that really make you feel better, Mother? Does knowing that Jim's in heaven console you at all? Do you feel special that God's testing you?

DOLORES: I think it's time for you to be quiet now, Joyce.

JOYCE: And then there was Mrs. d'Angelo. And that whole tapestry bullshit. What good is putting up with the knots and tangles if we don't get to see the finished product? God's got this beautiful design planned? *Show me!* If I like it, *then* I'll put up with all this shit! But right now, I don't give a fuck about God's plan.

DOLORES: Joyce!—

JOYCE: Stop pretending you aren't angry, Mother. You're human. Neither of us are saints, we're two ordinary people angry at God because he doesn't give a shit about us!

DOLORES: Shut up!—

JOYCE: No! I don't care! God can smite me with a lightning bolt, I don't give a damn. Fuck God, fuck the plan, fuck the tapestry, FUCK IT ALL!

>   *DOLORES slaps JOYCE. Beat. JOYCE smacks DOLORES to the ground.*

>   *Long pause.*

>   *JOYCE runs off.*

Scene 10

> *NICK's rectory. A knock at the door.*

NICK: Enter.

> *DOLORES enters, wearing a wrist brace.*

Good evening, Dolores. This is a pleasant surprise. *(Pause.)* What can I do for you. *(Pause.)* Would you like some tea?

DOLORES: Where's Joyce.

NICK: What do you mean "Where's Joyce."

DOLORES: She ran away. Where is she.

NICK: I wouldn't know.

DOLORES: She has to be somewhere, and I called all of her friends. I even called Noah Weisenthal.

NICK: Why did she run away?

DOLORES: Why do you think!

NICK: …I really don't know, Dolores—

DOLORES: You couldn't leave well enough alone. Joyce and I were coping just fine and you had to tear open old wounds and pour salt into them.

NICK: What happened. Did you fight?

DOLORES: Yes. We fought. And I've got the sprain to show for it. And I hold you entirely responsible.

NICK: What did I do?—

DOLORES: I am going to phone the Archbishop tomorrow and demand that you be transferred. You are a horrible priest and a disservice to this parish—

NICK: Dolores, calm down—

DOLORES: I will not calm down—

NICK: Please!—Before you have me excommunicated, let's just talk, okay? Can we do that? *(Pause.)* Now please, let's sit down. We'll have some tea.

DOLORES: I don't want tea.

NICK: Earl Grey, Orange Pekoe, English Breakfast?

DOLORES: …Darjeeling?

NICK: Done. *(Plops a bag into the pot.)*

DOLORES: Are you even dimly aware of the damage you've done?

NICK: I gave the best advice I could. I thought it would be good for her.

DOLORES: How can this be good?

NICK: Confronting the offender, expressing repressed feelings—

DOLORES: Don't give me that pamphlet talk, Father, I've never bought into it.

NICK: This is a method of restorative justice endorsed by many Christian churches, not the least of which is the Catholic Church.

DOLORES: I'm sick of hearing all these bleeding hearts within the Church showing mercy to criminals. What about us? Who showed us mercy?

NICK: You're not excluded—

DOLORES: Certainly not that killer. Certainly not the courts. Ten years? That's hardly enough.

NICK: Look, if you don't want to participate, you're free to make that choice. But Joyce is free to make her own choice too.

DOLORES: Joyce is easily manipulated.

NICK: That's hard to believe.

DOLORES: She pretends to be all brave and rebellious, but she's really in a very fragile state right now. And your manipulating her is not helping.

NICK: I am not manipulating her. What reason would I have.

DOLORES: To push your agenda, of course.

NICK: I have an agenda? This is news to me.

DOLORES: You will not last long in this parish, Father.

             Pause.

NICK: I am on your side, Dolores. I'm on your side and I'm on Joyce's side. I want both of you to be happy. Do you think I became a priest to mess with people's lives? To push some agenda?

             Come on. Do you honestly believe that I intend you or Joyce any sort of malice whatsoever? Yes or no.

DOLORES: …No.

NICK: Do you believe that I'm trying to help you. Yes or no.

DOLORES: …Yes.

NICK: But you don't think I'm doing a good job.

DOLORES: I think your efforts are misguided.

NICK: Okay. You're entitled to that. So now my job is to convince you that this is the Good Christian thing to do, or at least to get you thinking about it. Will you allow me to try.

             DOLORES nods assent.

             Thank you. Let's see now…showing mercy…okay, take Jesus on the cross. Two criminals crucified, one to his right and one to his left. One guy's cussing him out, the other guy's berating the first guy. And Jesus tells the other guy that even though he led a life of crime, that very day he will join him in paradise. And so it follows, QED.

DOLORES: But the other criminal was repentant.

NICK: Jesus must've given the first guy a sporting chance though, right?

DOLORES: Perhaps, but he rejected it.

NICK: But he gave him a chance. That's the important thing.

DOLORES: But he rejected it. That's the important thing.

NICK: ...Fine, that was a lame example anyway. Okay. Jesus on the cross again. He's on the wood, they're nailing spikes through his wrists. And even as the hammers are flailing away, what does he say? "Forgive them Father, for they know not what they do."

DOLORES: Only because Jesus understood that his crucifixion was necessary.

NICK: ...Okay, how about this—

DOLORES: Father. I know what you're trying to say. You believe that one must forgive unconditionally. But Michael Sawchuk has already been judged. By the courts and by God. Even if I were to show mercy, what use would it be? I can't change God's mind, can I?

NICK: There's no room at all for redemption?

DOLORES: ...No. The damage he's done to our lives... How can anyone be redeemed from that?

Jim had such promise, Father. He was going to be an engineer. Something he always wanted to be. He had a girlfriend, too. Beautiful young woman. He was going to marry her. After the incident, she just…disappeared…

Then of course there's me and Joyce. My husband died three years earlier of a heart attack, and just when we were getting over that…

I love my Joyce. She's all I have now. I can't let anything happen to her. You understand that.

I know what's best for her. And this is not. So I ask you Father, please, don't let her go through with this.

NICK: The choice is ultimately hers. I can't change that. And I can't change what I believe, either.

             Pause.

DOLORES: Has Joyce phoned you or come by here at all?

NICK: No.

DOLORES: Please phone me if you hear from her.

NICK: I will.

DOLORES: Thank you for the tea.

NICK: My pleasure.

             DOLORES starts to leave —

Wait!—

Okay. Jesus on the cross again. He's been hanging there for hours. At the foot of the cross is his mother Mary. This woman, seeing the fruit of her womb nailed, mutilated, bloodied and rejected. Her son had done so much for so many, changed the lives of thousands of people for the better, and this was the payoff for all that. Imagine the anger, the confusion, the hatred she must have felt. Now let me ask you… Did *she* forgive?

DOLORES: …probably not right away…

NICK: Eventually?

> *Pause.*

DOLORES: Please phone me.

> *DOLORES exits.*

> *JOYCE emerges from another room.*

NICK: She cares about you.

JOYCE: I know. I feel like shit.

NICK: Sit down. I'll make you some tea.

JOYCE: Would you give the tea thing a rest?—

NICK: Earl Grey, Orange Pekoe, English Breakfast?

JOYCE: …Orange Pekoe…

NICK: As you wish. *(Plops a bag into a mug.)*

> *NICK approaches JOYCE and sets the mug down in front of her. They both stare at it for a while.*

JOYCE: I'm a horrible daughter.

NICK: Don't say that.

JOYCE: I screamed at her. I pushed her to the ground. She sprained something?

NICK: Her wrist.

JOYCE: …God…

NICK: What happened, happened.

JOYCE: I love my mother, Nick.

NICK: I know you do.

JOYCE: …We're hurting each other…I hate this, why are we hurting each other…?

Pause.

NICK: Noah came by today. He dropped off a letter. Would you like to see it?

> *NICK takes a sealed envelope from a table and hands it to JOYCE. She opens it, and pulls out a one-page letter. She flips it over, and finds no other writing.*

JOYCE: This is it?

> *NICK shrugs. JOYCE reads the letter as NICK looks on.*

It reads like a business letter.

NICK: Were you expecting more?

JOYCE: Well yeah. I was expecting…I dunno…

NICK: A soul-wrenching aria of self-abasing contrition?

JOYCE: …Well yeah. *(Reads.)* "I look forward to meeting you." Like it's some kind of parent-teacher interview. *(Pause.)* Is this really a good idea?

NICK: You know where I stand.

JOYCE: Yeah I know, healing process, blah blah blah. Very therapeutic. But this isn't just about therapy. I can see that now. This is about right and wrong. This is about damage done. And there's a lot of damage, Nick. A lot. Am I going to ignore all that damage just so I can feel better?

NICK: Of course not. That would be denial.

JOYCE: Then why should I do this.

NICK: Because it's right.

JOYCE: …Because it's the Good Christian Thing.

NICK: Sure.

JOYCE: *(Beat.)* It's amazing how you can stand in front of those people every week and keep a straight face.

NICK: Now, Joyce, you're not turning cynical on me, are you?

JOYCE: Me? God forbid!

They sit in silence for a while. JOYCE sips her tea.

You never gave me a straight answer. When I asked where your doubting led you.

NICK: I told you, it led me here. That's as straight as I can get.

JOYCE: Care to elaborate?

NICK: ...no, not really.

JOYCE: Touchy subject. Does it have to do with Saint Jude?

NICK: Maybe.

JOYCE: Does it have to do with your prison ministry?

NICK: Is this Twenty Questions?

JOYCE: If you want it to be.

NICK: ...I don't.

They sit. JOYCE sips her tea.

JOYCE: Do you believe in Heaven?

NICK: Probably.

JOYCE: I think I believe in Heaven. We're supposed to be living in this secular, rational age, but I can't stop believing in it, I can't stop *wanting* to.

I talk to Jim sometimes. Not like praying or anything, I just talk. He had a quick wit. I was pretty fast, but Jim...comebacks, put-downs, he was an artist. He doesn't say much anymore. Maybe that's why we invented Heaven. So we can get in the last word.

NICK: Or maybe he finally learned the art of listening.

JOYCE: Maybe. *(Beat.)* I just want to know what happened to him. If I'll ever see him again.

I didn't even get to say goodbye. He was just—cut off. All that potential, all that stuff that could have been. He deserved to live, Nick, he deserved a shot at living, at being happy, but he didn't get one 'cause that *asshole* cut him off!—

She spills tea on herself.

Shit!

NICK: Are you okay?

JOYCE: Fuck that hurt!

NICK: Are you burned?

JOYCE: No, no, just scalded me a little, I'm fine. Ow.

NICK: You sure?

JOYCE: If not, you'll hear from my lawyer.

NICK: Lemme get that spill— *(Grabs a towel and starts dabbing.)*

JOYCE: My hand's turning a pretty shade of red. Shit, I got it all over my sweater.

NICK: Want me to pop it in the wash?

JOYCE: No, it's okay—

NICK: I was gonna do a load anyway. Give it here.

Pause. JOYCE slips off the sweater, revealing a bare-shouldered top underneath. She gives the sweater to NICK, and continues to nurse her hand. NICK's attention is riveted to JOYCE's bare shoulders and back, where the scars from her bullet wounds are still visible.

JOYCE gradually becomes aware of NICK's gaze.

JOYCE: *(Never looking at him.)* Getting shot is a surreal experience. Not much pain, really. Just an overwhelming sense of dread. The pain comes later, when you're writhing in a hospital bed and hitting that morphine button like you're on Jeopardy. I had some great hallucinations, though. The cast of ER came into my room and had a tea party.

Long pause.

NICK: I'll throw this in the wash.

NICK goes to leave—

JOYCE: Nick.

NICK: Yes?

JOYCE: How long would it take to set up a meeting with Michael Sawchuk?

Pause.

NICK: ...Well...I'd have to talk with the program director...there's no guarantee that Sawchuk's ready to meet with you—

JOYCE: Could you look into it for me?

NICK: ...Sure... Don't you want to carry on with the correspondence for a while though? Ease into it?—

JOYCE: Letters are a waste of time. I'm ready to see him now.

NICK: ...Okay... First thing in the morning. I'll make some calls.

JOYCE: Thank you.

NICK leaves. JOYCE is alone.

…there are some things that need to be said out loud…

Fade out.

Scene 11

Spot on JOYCE, seated.

JOYCE: Never thought you'd see me again, did you?

Same here. If someone told me that one day I'd be sitting across a table from you…

You look good. Nice outfit. Not many people can pull off orange, but on you…

All right…to business…

Two years ago…something happened that changed a lot of people's lives. Irrevocably. That means you can't change it back. And I can safely say that everyone is worse off for it. My brother's dead— can't get any worse off than that. It certainly hasn't done you any favours. And me…well, my life's gone to shit.

It's gotten marginally better recently. I can step out of the house without going catatonic now, thank you very much. But I still have nightmares. Usually there's some surreal twist to nightmares, but mine are pretty straightforward. Just plays that night over and over again. In mind-numbing detail. The flicker of the fluorescent lights. Racks of Cheetos and potato chips. Jim telling me he might have gotten Rachel pregnant. To this day I don't know if I'm an aunt or not. You bursting in with your blue balaclava. People screaming. The rhythm of your gunshots. The sharp, weird feeling of bullets ripping through me. The speckled dirt on the floor.

The taste of the floor. Jim's body next to mine as we both bled on the floor...

My nightmares are boring, but they're thorough.

Do you have any nightmares? Do you wake up in a cold sweat? Screaming in your bed? Does the guard have to come and tell you to shut up?

How *is* life in the big house, Mr. Sawchuk? You eating right? Getting lots of exercise? I hear you've got a lounge and a rec room and a gym—it's like Club Med in here. Are you behaving yourself? That's really important, you know. Four years till parole, that's a long stretch of time to be a good boy. You think you can swing it?

Sorry. I'm being facetious. That means I'm kidding in a mean way.

This meeting is supposed to be about healing old wounds. Yours and mine. I know I have my wounds. You gave them to me. Where are yours? You've done nothing to show me you have them. I remember you in court last year. Your face. Not the slightest hint of remorse. Not the slightest pang of guilt. And right now. Right in front of me. A complete poker face. And look at you. You're fit, clean shaven, eating three squares a day, basketball in the afternoon—Is this punishment? Is this atonement? You're getting out in five to ten. I have to live with this my whole life! And you dare to ask *me* to help heal *you*? From what!

I hate you, Michael Sawchuk. You're an evil, conscienceless monster. You're a mistake. You never should have been born. And if there's a Hell, and I hope to God there is, nothing would warm my heart more than to see you burn.

A door opens behind her.

Lights up to full to reveal a hallway just outside the

door of a prison meeting room. NICK steps out of the room into the hallway.

NICK: Well. He says he's ready. Are you?

JOYCE: …Yeah…

NICK: Are you sure you want to do this?

JOYCE: Yes. I'm here, I travelled all this way, I will do this.

NICK: Just remember why we're here. To start a dialogue. To communicate. That's all.

JOYCE: Right.

NICK: Do you know what you're going to say to him?

JOYCE: You bet.

NICK: All right. Let's go.

            NICK opens the door. JOYCE slowly approaches, but quickly sits back down, agitated.

            (To Sawchuk.) We'll be with you shortly. *(Closes the door.)* If you're having second thoughts—

JOYCE: No… If I don't do this now, I'm never gonna do it.

NICK: You don't have to.

JOYCE: Why the hell are you doing an about-face on this! I thought you wanted this to happen!

NICK: I did, but only under the right conditions. We're only here because you insisted you were ready and I trusted you.

JOYCE: I *am* ready, lemme just— *(Takes some deep breaths, calms down.)* …I caught a glimpse of him. I saw half his body through the door frame.

NICK: How'd he look to you.

JOYCE: He looked… He was wearing a T-shirt and jeans.

NICK: You thought he'd be wearing an orange jumpsuit or something?

JOYCE: Okay— ...*(Breathes.)* Okay, let's get in there.

NICK: You sure?

JOYCE: Yes.

             JOYCE rises and walks with NICK into the room. The stage is empty for a while. Then JOYCE bursts out of the room, profoundly disturbed. NICK follows.

             JOYCE tries desperately to calm herself down.

NICK: What's wrong.

JOYCE: I feel like I'm gonna puke.

NICK: Okay, just breathe—

JOYCE: Oh God—just—this flash! of— ...I felt like screaming... I wasn't going to ...not in front of him—

NICK: The guard's waving at me. What the hell does he want.

JOYCE: It just came all at once!

NICK: Something's up, I have to see what it is.

JOYCE: Where are you going?

NICK: Don't worry, I won't be long. Sit tight. And whatever you do, don't enter that room without me.

             NICK exits. JOYCE is left alone, trying and failing to regain her composure.

JOYCE: ...fuck...fuck...Fuck fuck fuck— ... *(Looks at her shaking hand, tries to keep it still.)*

             You're not gonna do this to me... It's supposed to be my turn now... MY TURN!... *(Sinks to the floor.)*

Look at me! I can't win, I can't win! ...Are you happy? I'm on the fucking *floor*, are you happy now?

...God ...I wish I died that night...

DOLORES: Don't say that.

> *DOLORES has entered. JOYCE stares at her for a while.*

JOYCE: ...Why are you—

DOLORES: It was an open invitation. *(Pause.)* Have you gone in yet?

JOYCE: ...not really...

DOLORES: We're going home.

JOYCE: ...No!...

DOLORES: *We're going home.*

JOYCE: Mother, I'm going to do this—

DOLORES: No. This has gone too far. I'm sick of being told "it's her choice, it's her choice." Well now it's my choice. I'm making it my choice. I am your mother and you are coming with me. *(Grabs her daughter off the floor.)*

JOYCE: No, you don't understand—

DOLORES: Don't argue with me—

JOYCE: *(Tries to break free.)* —Mother let me go—

DOLORES: —No—

JOYCE: —Mother please—

DOLORES: —I'm taking you out if I have to wrestle you out—

JOYCE: —you're hurting me!—

DOLORES: —Come with me!

JOYCE: No!

DOLORES: *Joyce come with me!*

JOYCE: You're hurting me!—

             *As they struggle, NICK dashes in and separates
             them.*

NICK: Stop it! Both of you!

DOLORES: Stay out of this, Father.

JOYCE: *(Nursing her wrist.)* Ow!

NICK: Dolores, stop it!

DOLORES: Let go of me—

NICK: Stop it!

             *DOLORES and NICK struggle. DOLORES'
             sprained wrist acts up, she flinches painfully, breaks
             free and retreats.*

             *DOLORES and JOYCE are in their respective
             corners, nursing their injuries, with NICK in the
             middle. Long pause.*

DOLORES: Aren't we a sight. Are you happy now, Father? Is
             this the way you wanted to help us?

JOYCE: Leave him alone.

DOLORES: Do you see now what you've done to us? That's my
             daughter over there, I just injured her, *I* did, her
             own mother. You know how that makes me feel?
             No, of course not. You don't care. All you care about
             is the program, how great it is, how therapeutic.

NICK: Dolores—

DOLORES: And at the end of it all, where are we?

NICK: Do you honestly think you could have gone on the
             way you were?

DOLORES: Anything is better than this! What good has this done us?

NICK: Listen to yourself, putting the blame everywhere except— …This is not about the program. The program did not do this. This is about you.

JOYCE: Nick, don't—

NICK: This is about you and your denial and your failure to meet your daughter's needs in her grief.

DOLORES: I helped my daughter! Every step. I was the one that sat vigil by her bedside while she was in the hospital. I was the one that stood by her at the funeral as we buried her brother. I was the one that came running to her bedroom every time she woke up in a screaming cold sweat. That was all me!

            And what do I get in return.

            Can you answer that, Joyce?

            Pause.

            Please come home with me.

JOYCE: …not yet.

DOLORES: Why.

NICK: Because she knows the value of this.

DOLORES: I wasn't talking to you.

NICK: This process works for many people, Dolores. But since you refuse to give it a chance, I can only hope that you learn from your daughter's example. She's about to do something that will forward her Christian life greatly. She's going into that room and she's going to start the process of reconciliation.

JOYCE: …No, I'm not.

            Mother. If you had the chance to look Michael

Sawchuk in the eye and say anything you want to him, what's the first thing you would say? Certainly not "I forgive you."

He's expecting me to help him heal. He's getting something else. He made us suffer, Mother. We're still suffering. We're not getting any better. Why should he?

I'm sorry I lied to you, Nick. I know this isn't the Good Christian Thing. But to me, it's the right thing. He has to feel pain. And if he's in there all broken and begging to be healed, if he thinks he's got one foot in Hell already— ...I think it's within my right to give him a little push.

Pause.

NICK: If you're so keen on playing the avenging angel, why are you having such a tough time staying in that room?

JOYCE: Because I don't think I can face him alone. Now I won't have to.

You can come with me, Mother.

Pause.

DOLORES: He's in there right now.

JOYCE: Yes.

Pause.

NICK: Joyce. This isn't the reason we came.

JOYCE: It's exactly the reason we came. Expressing repressed feelings, right?

NICK: But the way you're doing it is destructive!

JOYCE: Gosh, I sure hope so!

NICK: Joyce, please, don't do this.

Silence from JOYCE.

…Dolores…

Pause.

DOLORES: This is no longer an issue of doing good or repairing damage done. My son dies for no good reason and I'm left to deal with it for the rest of my life. There's something very unsatisfying about that, Father.

NICK: Dolores…right now, you've got a chance to achieve something creative. Something that bears witness to God.

DOLORES: Don't speak to me about God.

NICK: You can't turn your back on a lifetime of devotion to your Church.

DOLORES: I can't turn my back on my son's memory! I am not going to let him die in vain.

NICK: Joyce…please…

JOYCE: I'm sorry, Nick.

Pause.

NICK stations himself at the door.

NICK: Well I won't let you.

JOYCE: Step away from the door.

NICK: No.

JOYCE: Stop playing the fucking bouncer, Nick, step away from the door!

NICK: No.

JOYCE: Let us through the goddamn door! *(Tries to force her way through.)*

NICK: *(Fending her off.)* No!

JOYCE: Mother help me!

DOLORES joins in the fray. They struggle ridiculously for control of the doorknob until—

NICK: THAT'S IT!! Stop it!! Both of you! Sit down!

DOLORES and JOYCE are a bit stunned.

I Said Sit Down.

DOLORES and JOYCE obey.

I know you're angry. I know you wanna tear that asshole in there limb from limb but I won't let you do it! Because like it or not, no matter how vile or unredeemable you may think he is, that man is a human being. That man is a Child of God.

JOYCE: …Jesus Christ…

NICK: This is extremely hard for you, I know. But this hasn't been easy for me, either.

JOYCE: What the hell do *you* have at stake? Up until now, all you've done was harp on about doing the "Good Christian Thing". Just because everything was all sunshine and roses in your fucking prison ministry you think it'll be the same here?

NICK: …It wasn't.

Pause.

There was this one inmate. A sex offender. Wayne Scrivener. He and I used to joke about the name Wayne; he was doomed to the criminal life from birth. He was doing really well, on track with all his rehab programs, really cleaned himself up. When his parole came up, I couldn't sing his praises any louder. I told the board unequivocally that he was fully rehabilitated with zero chance of re-offending. So they let him go. A few weeks later, he rapes and tortures a girl to death, then kills himself. Saint Jude finds out I was the one that gave him the clean bill of health, they make up all kinds of horrible legends about me...and here I am.

I want you to know something. You two ladies are the best thing that's ever happened to me. I've grown to care about you two a lot. And it's not fair that two women—two strong, passionate, good-hearted women—can have such a horrible thing happen to them. Anyone else could turn all fatalistic and declare the rule of Chaos and the death of God and all that, but I can't. I'm not allowed to. I'm a priest.

That's why you're here. You're here to prove that it can still work. That I'm not wasting my life chasing some two-thousand-year-old pipe dream.

Pause. NICK looks at the door, then steps away from it, relinquishing control.

Silence.

DOLORES gets up, walks slowly to the door, and stares at it for a long while. She puts her hand out to JOYCE, who rises, walks to her mother and takes her hand. DOLORES opens the door slowly. They both walk in.

The door shuts. NICK is alone in a chair. He buries his face in his hands.

Silence.

After only a moment, JOYCE and DOLORES emerge from the room, solemn and thoughtful. Pause.

DOLORES: What kind of prison is this. He's not even wearing orange.

NICK: What happened.

DOLORES: ...Nothing...We stared at him...He stared back...We left.

JOYCE: He just sat there. Staring at us. He looked— resigned. Like he was expecting it. My mind went blank.

Defeated silence all around.

NICK: Well, should we pack up and go home? Or would you like to stare at him some more?

JOYCE: ...I don't know... Mother?

DOLORES: I'm not sure...

NICK: Make up your mind. I can't leave unless you do. I'm sick of this place.

Pause.

JOYCE: I'm sorry I lied to you.

NICK: So am I.

JOYCE: You'll never trust me again.

NICK: Probably not.

Pause.

JOYCE: You really believe in it, don't you.

NICK: I have no choice. *(Pause.)* You spend all your time preaching how God is present in all things, works through all things. And you look around and... *(Trails off.)* Doesn't help much in the way of career satisfaction. *(Pause.)* It works. I know it works. I just want to see it for myself. Just once.

JOYCE: ...I hope you will, someday. You have a good vision. It's noble. I admire it.

NICK turns to her.

I do. But I'm gonna need time. And help. *(Beat.)*

You're not about to leave the priesthood over this, are you?

NICK: I couldn't leave if I wanted to. It's like the mob that way.

JOYCE: You're a good priest.

NICK: Thanks. 'Course if I did leave, you're the only person who'd miss me.

JOYCE: That's not true.

NICK: What do you have to say, Dolores?

DOLORES: ...I'm sorry?

NICK: Should I leave the priesthood or should I stay?

DOLORES: Well...there is a shortage, after all.

NICK: Ever the pragmatist.

DOLORES: Joyce.

JOYCE: Yes?

DOLORES: ...We're not well.

            Silence.

JOYCE: ...I know.

            Pause.

NICK: Is this something you'd like to do privately? ...'Cause, in case you forgot, we've got a guy in there who's been waiting for some time to speak with you. Would you like to call this off or...

JOYCE: Mother? What do you think.

DOLORES: I don't know...

JOYCE: Give us a minute, Nick.

NICK: Sure. I guess I can go in there and entertain the poor guy. I'll tell him some Jesuit jokes.

(Goes to the door.) You'll be okay?

JOYCE: I think we will, yeah.

NICK enters the room and closes the door.

JOYCE: He's in there, Mother.

DOLORES: Yes he is.

JOYCE: He might help.

DOLORES: He could.

Silence.

You're a beautiful girl.

JOYCE: ...Why did you say that.

DOLORES: I don't know. Because you are.

Pause.

Joyce...can you ever—

JOYCE: ...Yes. I can... Can you?...

Pause. Fade out.

The End.

pyg

Rose Condo

Set

The set consists of the following: a screen placed upstage centre, a mannequin stage left of the screen, a large mime box and two small mime boxes. The mime boxes will be used to represent the different locations of the play.

1.

A YOUNG WOMAN enters and stands in front of the screen. She wears casual clothing—possibly a zip up sweater and plain pants. She wears glasses and her hair is in a ponytail.

Hi. How are you? My name is—oh, right, we're not supposed to say our names. Well, um, I'm number 57513. That's 5…7…5…1…3.

Pause.

My interests include reading books and watching movies. I like to cook. I'm a pretty good cook. I like to walk. I like going for walks.

Pause.

When I said just now that I'm a good cook, I just meant that I can cook a few things really well. Not gourmet. Just, you know, good.

Pause.

I like going to museums. I really like looking at art and just, you know, getting lost in the art.

Pause.

Sorry, it's just that, um, when I said that I can, well, that I can cook, I didn't mean that I eat a lot. It's not like all I do is eat.

Pause.

You know that saying about the camera adds…

I'd like to meet you. I think that would be really great. I forgot to mention, I really like watching sports—like football. I know what a "penalty-offside-first-down-repeated" means. And if you like football too, we could watch games together, if you wanted.

And I don't have a cat…in case you're allergic.

I have a car.

I have a job, but I'm not like super busy with it. You know, flexible schedule. I work as a tele-sales representative—which is just a fancy way of saying I'm a telemarketer. Outbound. Maybe your number has been on my call list, and I've called you, and we've already had a conversation.

    Pause.

So my number again is 57513. And, um…I'd like to meet you.

    She smiles.

2.

    She is sitting at a bar.

So here I am, at this bar called Ignite. I'm waiting for number 48612 to show up. Friday night.

    She looks at the door, sips her drink, looks around, looks at the door, sips her drink, looks around.

It's not a blind date. I've already seen him in his video.

The bartender has seen me here a couple of times before, and he talked to me for a little while. He got pretty busy, though. There are these really big-breasted girls sitting at the other end of the bar.

    Pause.

I figured out that my number, 57513 and his number, 48612 both added up to 21.

I can't remember if we had said to meet at 7:00 or 7:30—which actually doesn't matter since it's a quarter after eight.

Wrestling is on TV. This bald man in a silk suit is making out with this female wrestler. Everyone is cheering…

> *She looks at the door, sips her drink, looks around, looks at the door, sips her drink, looks around.*

I'll go as soon as my drink is done.

> *Pause.*

Someone sits down beside me—grey suit, comb over, cigarette hanging off his lip, totally staring at me. Not number 48612. If I stay absolutely still, he'll lose interest and go away. Go away. Go away. I take a sip of my drink and some spills on my chest. Shit. Don't look down.

> *She twirls her hair and tries to cover the spilt drink on her chest. She crosses her legs away from "him."*

I wish I had something to read, someone to talk to. Any time, 48612. Now would be perfect. Can't he tell I'm waiting for someone? He probably thinks I'm some loser sitting by herself. Or maybe he thinks I'm one of those pathetic women who go alone to bars to get picked up by some guy. I can be interested in something. I can watch wrestling. The TV is right above his head. Fuck! I made eye contact. Look away. Don't move.

He speaks to me.

He asked if I want another drink, because I'm wearing my first one.

(To him.) No thank you.

He's yelling at me.

He just called me a bitch.

He's gone.

The bartender comes over.

He asked if I want another drink.

> *She shakes her head no.*

He asked if I'm okay.

> *She nods her head yes.*

He asked if I gave that guy my phone number.

> *She shakes her head no.*

(*To the audience.*) I need to be out of here.

(*To the bartender.*) It's getting late. I think I'm going to head home.

He laughed and said it's not even midnight.

(*To the bartender.*) Yeah, well, I'm tired. Gotta get up early in the morning. Feed my cat. Anyway, bye.

> *She changes the set to be her couch at home. She brings the mirror on stage.*

(*To the audience.*) I'm not tired. I don't have to get up early. I don't have a cat.

> *She hangs her sweater on the mannequin, and takes off her shoes.*

This is the last time I take any dating advice from anyone. I've done the blind date, the set-up, the surprise set-up—"oh have you met my friend so-and-so? He works in communications too…" Blah blah blah.

If 48612 had shown up, the grey suit guy wouldn't

have said anything to me. If I had been some gorgeous, big-breasted bar girl, that guy wouldn't have had the balls to come near me. And if he had, I would have had the balls to tell him to get lost. And I would have ordered another drink and flirted with the bartender. I probably could have gotten the bartender's number. I bet I coulda been having sex with the bartender right now.

Pause.

It's okay though. I'm going through this thing right now where I just need to watch TV. By myself.

She picks up a remote and turns the TV on.

The following is pre-recorded.

"...With this fantastic new product, you can actually lose weight while you chew your food."

She changes the channel.

(Southern accent.) "I just want to tell my sister that I'm sorry I slept with her boyfriend." *(New York accent.)* "Okay, audience. Should we bring the sister out here?" *(The audience cheers.)*

She changes the channel.

(Elvis Presley sings "Are you Lonesome Tonight.") "Are you stuck in a rut? Do you need to meet new and exciting people?" *(The music changes to something techno.)* "Then call now! 1-800-HOTT-FUN and get connected. Find friendship, fun times and maybe even romance. That's 1-800-HOTT-FUN. *(Super fast.)* $4.99 per minute. Must be over 18. HOTT FUN does not screen its callers and discourages meeting in person."

She changes the channel.

"Watch as 25 women battle it out for the attentions of one man. Stay tuned to witness the agony, the tears, the catfights and the jewellery. Who will survive to be his one true love?"

She changes the channel.

(Pachelbel's "Canon" plays.) "As you walk down the aisle, a new chapter of your life begins. Let us help make your wedding day a special day…"

She changes the channel.

"Looking to meet that special someone? Then book now with Sail-a-Mate Cruise Lines. Ride the high seas with hundreds of other singles, just like yourself! Enjoy sun by day, and fun by night. There's plenty of entertainment, lots of great food, and ladies? You drink for free!"

She turns the TV off.

I used to imagine what life would be like when I was older—living in my own apartment. Having the freedom to do whatever I wanted. Having fun, partying all night. Having sex. Having lots of sex with lots of different people.

She looks at her watch.

I should go to bed.

I don't want to go to bed. Lie in that big empty bed all by myself. I want someone there—lying next to me. A warm body beside me. He will wrap his arms around me and spoon me. He'll stare at me while I'm sleeping. He'll kiss my eyelids, and listen to my heart beating. He'll want to make love all night. He'll tell me again and again how beautiful I am.

And then…

I'm not really here. This is not really happening to me. This is not my life. It can't be.

I'm supposed to be in my prime—experiencing…

things. Men. I'm deep into my twenties and I'm still single. Soon I'll be thirty. Then I'll be forty. And then, before I know it, I'll be dried up, expired, still single and forced to sit on the Internet all day just so I can have some human contact.

I'm not good on my own.

People tell me I should get a cat. Apparently cats are good companions. I hate cats. I hate cats because they shed, their pee stinks, and I'm in my twenties. I don't want to cuddle in bed with a cat. I could turn into one of those cat-obsessed women—who surround themselves with cat calendars and cat bookmarks and cat tea cozies and Christmas cards with pictures of me and my cat.

No. No. I am above that.

I am fine on my own. I am independent. I don't need anyone.

You hear that, Mr Mysterious Future Love of my Life?

I have erotic books and a vibrator.

I don't need you.

I'm not even looking for you.

Pause.

"Love will come along when you least expect it."

Okay. So I'm not looking. I'm ready.

Anytime now, I just know it, I'll be walking out my front door, or in Safeway, or renting a movie, or going to work, or at work, or checking my mail, or filling up at a gas station, or in the laundromat, or out with friends, or at a coffee shop, or at a bar, or picking up Chinese food, or in the waiting room at the dentist, or in the library, or picking up dry-cleaning, and BOOM! There you'll be. Totally out of the blue. I won't have seen it coming. And there I'll be. And I'll just, you know, I'll know. That it's you, and you're…it. Tag. You're it. Betcha can't catch me. You'll never find me. Find me. Come on. Where are you?

Pause.

I've got so much to offer!

She yawns.

I've got so much to offer…

She pauses and sleepily looks around. She takes off her glasses and rubs her eyes. She takes her hair out of the ponytail.

I've got a job. I've got an apartment. I've got cable.

She continues mumbling as she walks off stage.

3.

Morning music plays.

She enters wearing casual pants and a bathrobe. She isn't wearing her glasses. She yawns and stretches. She puts lotion on her face, combs her hair and puts on her glasses. She looks at herself in the mirror. The music stops abruptly.

I wish—

It doesn't matter.

She puts clips in her hair and puts it in a ponytail.

I'm not—

If I were number 48612, I would see me, and think …

Pause.

Who am I kidding?

She cleans her ears with cotton swabs and looks again in the mirror.

Honestly? Honestly. I...am...pathetic. Boring. I'm so boring. I look boring. Plain. Who's going to look at me—this, and think, "Hey! She's hot! She's someone I want to—"

She stops.

There's gotta be something...

She takes her hair out of a ponytail and shakes it.

...something I can do...to stand out.

She slowly unties her bathrobe.

To get noticed.

She unties her bathrobe to reveal she's wearing a plain, unsupportive sports bra. She lifts each breast and pushes them together and looks in the mirror.

Oh my God.

I...had no idea. I could. I mean, it's possible.

Hello? Number 48612? It's so nice to meet you.

No, I don't want another drink. I'm waiting for someone. Get lost asshole.

Yes, I'm 57513. What's that? You think I'm beautiful? Well, I hear that a lot, but it's the most special coming from you.

She looks at her watch. She cleans up her "mess" and puts glasses on. She leaves her hair down and puts on a sweater that zips all the way up to her chin. She looks at herself, and after a moment she unzips the sweater part way.

Perfect.

4.

She stands centre stage clutching an armful of beauty magazines.

I can be so judgmental.

I always thought these were a waste of money. Eye candy for men waiting in line at the supermarket. But today I looked closer, and I discovered that these magazines are full of information.

She lays the magazines around her and reads the headlines.

"Five tips for successful flirting."

Perfect.

"Panty personality—from granny gitch to teensy thong, what you wear down there says a lot about you."

She feels her bum for her panty line and groans.

"Make him moan—Six tips to drive his shaft into high gear."

"Workplace passion—True Confessions of luscious ladies who bang their bosses."

I don't know where to start. Horoscope?

She closes her eyes and randomly points to one magazine.

Okay.

She flips to the horoscope page.

Gemini. Here we go.

"This month you are working towards the achievement of a goal. Work hard. Give it your all."

Wow, that's...I need a second opinion.

She closes her eyes and points to another magazine. She flips to the horoscope page.

Gemini. Okay.

"This month, leave all big projects aside and focus on having fun. Your social life will be rewarded."

Hmm.

She looks at both horoscopes, and tosses the second one aside.

Okay, then. Give it my all.

She looks at other magazines.

Give it my all.

She picks up one magazine.

"How lust-worthy are you? Find out your lust level in our red-hot, lust-acular quiz."

Perfect.

She flips to the quiz.

Number 1…A.

Number 2…C.

Number 3…Um, none of the above.

Number 4…B, I guess

Number 5…B…and D.

Okay. *(She reads.)* "Total up your points from each question using this lust-rated chart."

She does so.

Ten points. *(She reads.)* "If you scored 0…10 points, your lust level rates a kamikaze cold fish."

Okay.

(She reads.) "You shy away from lust-busting opportunities, preferring instead to dangle as a wallflower. 'Women in this category tend to have self-esteem issues,' explains Dr. Thurston Hughes, author of 'Putting the You in You Can Do It.' 'These women need to put themselves out there more and create a lust-quality all their own. Don't be afraid to give it your all.'"

I guess that explains a few things.

She turns a couple of pages in the magazine.

Maybe I hold back. Maybe I've got to let go.

She turns a couple more pages.

That is a nice dress. I wonder if I could…no. Too revealing. I could never…

Pause. She starts to carefully tear the page out of the magazine. After a moment, she rips the page out.

Perfect.

She flips a page.

Another perfect dress.

Rips page.

Perfect hair.

Rips page.

Perfect shoes.

Rips page.

It's all here. I've got it all right here.

She gathers up her magazines.

Flirting tips. Panty Personality. Make him moan. I can let loose. I can put myself out there. I can give it my all.

5.

She brings a large red shopping bag on stage. She begins her yoga routine.

I've never felt so healthy. I'm on a no-carb, glucose-free diet. "Say Good-bye to Saddlebags" says to cut out any food that your body would transform into fat or sugar. I can eat plain yogurt, broccoli, asparagus, spinach, tuna, lots of things. It's fun to organize a weekly meal plan, so that I don't have to obsess about food. I can focus on more important things—like my new fitness regimen. Every day—an hour of high-impact aerobics, twenty minutes of weight-lifting, twenty minutes on the stationary bike and twenty minutes of yoga—to keep me balanced. It's been three days, and I feel so...

I'm like a sponge. There's so much that I didn't know. I was so...oblivious. I'm taking it all in.

Plus...

She picks up the shopping bag.

I've created the perfect look. Dress. Shoes. Underwear.

Tonight is the night. I'm going to Ignite and I'm putting it all to the test.

Pause.

I have everything I need for the new perfect me.

But first...I need a visual.

She places the shopping bag centre stage. She rolls the mannequin centre stage. She takes a black thong out of the bag and puts it on the figure. She puts a black bra on the figure and stuffs it with magazine pages. She pulls a skimpy red dress out of the bag and slips it on the figure. She takes a moment looking at the figure, then grabs the bag and goes behind the screen. We see her throw her pants and bra in the air. We hear excited noises and grunts from her. She emerges from behind the screen wearing what the figure wears and carrying high-heeled shoes. She walks past the figure to the mirror where she puts the shoes on. Pause.

If I build it, he will come.

She adjusts her breasts in the push-up bra.

6.

She enters wearing a bathrobe and carrying a bag of potato chips. She opens the bag and starts stuffing chips into her mouth.

God, I'm starving.

She shoves more chips in her mouth. She realizes how much noise she's making, and looks offstage towards her bedroom. She carefully closes the chip bag and tries to chew quieter.

(With mouth full.) He's asleep.

But he's here. There's a man in my bed. *(She giggles.)* I did it.

She brushes crumbs off herself, picks chip bits out of her teeth and looks offstage again.

So there I was. Back at Ignite. No sign of the illusive 48612, but I didn't care. The bartender didn't even recognize me. He gave me a free drink. And *(Proudly.)* he stared at my boobs. A lot.

I sat at a table across from an empty chair. "Communicating Confidence" stresses that "when you walk into a room of strangers, put out the vibe. Conduct yourself in a way that says 'Boys, don't be afraid to strike out. Come and step up to the plate.'" So I sat there, putting out the vibe.

And then I saw HIM. Staring at me. And I stared back. He smiled. So I smiled. And I looked at the empty chair beside me, and he was on his way over. He looked nice. Nice clothes. No grey hair. No comb over. No wedding ring. He sat down and started talking.

She closes her eyes.

From my research, I had made a list of what to do in a situation like this. I saw the list in my head, and I remembered everything...

eye contact

laugh

toss my hair

touch his arm

cross my legs toward him

cross my arms and squeeze my boobs

lick my lips.

It went over really well. He was really into me. And he was so nice. He bought me a couple of drinks. We both laughed a lot. It was like, instant connection. As soon as he started talking, he wasn't interested in anything else. He was totally focussed on me. And he stared at my boobs. A lot.

So he talked for a while, and then he got up to leave, and he asked if I wanted to come over for a drink. At his apartment. Oh. God.

Pause.

"Picture Perfect Pick-Up's" said that it's better to bring him home with you, so that you're on more familiar territory. So we came back here. I should have had another drink. We sat here. He talked. I really tried to focus on what he was saying, but all I could think was

"Should we have sex here or on my bed?"

"How does my hair look?"

"Does my breath smell?"

"Does my crotch smell?"

I wondered if he would go down on me. I imagined me going down on him.

And then I suddenly remembered the first time I heard the term oral sex. I was twelve, and I thought it meant talking really dirty. And I remembered health class, and the anonymous question day— where you write down the sex question you're too embarrassed to ask out loud, and you fold up your paper and put it in a box, and the teacher reads each one out loud, and answers all of them, and no one has to know what you wrote. So I wrote, "What is oral sex?" Mine was the last question. The teacher read it, and looked at the class and started to laugh. And the rest of the class laughed. So I laughed. And she said, "I think everyone can figure that one out."

It took me a while to figure that one out.

I wondered if he was expecting it, and was planning how he could maneuver his hand up behind my neck and gently pull me towards his...

Pause.

I realized I probably looked like I wasn't paying attention to HIM, so I licked my lips, tossed my hair and touched his leg all at once. He gave me a weird look, and I knew he thought I was a freak, so I grabbed him and I kissed him.

I know that "Six Steps to Seduction" stresses that "you have to let him make the first move." But

"Find the Tiger Inside" says that men get turned on by aggressive women. And it worked. We kissed. And kissed and kissed. He told me to relax. He asked where the bedroom was. He took my hand, and he led me into my bedroom. It was dark—I kept the lights off. He took my clothes off and took his clothes off. He lay me on my bed. I could only see the shape of him. But I could feel—his skin on my skin. He kissed my neck, my shoulders, my everywhere—he was everywhere—on me, inside of me, and it was so amazing …

And then he came.

He asked if his car would be okay overnight, and he rolled over and fell asleep.

I wanted to lie there with him. Naked. Together. But my room is hot, and I couldn't get comfortable. It's weird having someone else in my bed.

Pause.

It takes time, I guess. It takes time for two people to develop a sense of closeness. And find real, intimate connections. I read that in "Securing a Soul-Mate."

She finds his tie on the couch.

I just remembered…I said, "I like your tie." And he said, "I like your eyes." And we laughed because it rhymed.

She smiles.

He likes my eyes.

She lies down on the couch holding his tie. She yawns.

I wonder what he takes in his coffee. I hope I have milk.

7.

Morning music plays. She is asleep on the couch. She rolls over and sits up, yawning and stretching. She is sitting on something—it is the tie. She looks at it. She remembers what happened the night before, and rushes offstage.

Good morning. Wakey-wakey…. Hello?

A moment later she enters, wearing her glasses and holding a note. She sits on the couch.

(*She reads.*) "Had to run. Didn't want to wake you. Last night was great. I'll call you."

Pause. She sits on the couch.

Dammit. Why didn't he stay?

Pause.

Shit! It's because I slept out here. I know it. I wasn't going to sleep the whole night out here. I was just gonna lie here for a few minutes. I should've stayed awake. Oh shit. He thinks I didn't want him here. I wasn't avoiding him! He thinks I'm not attracted to him. I was! I totally was! We had a good time. No, we had a great time! He asked for my number even before we came back here. "Ten Hints that He's Hot for You" says that is a major sign that he's interested in seeing me again. He gave me his number too. Where did I—where is it? What did I—shit!

She runs behind the screen and appears holding his number.

Okay. Okay. This must—this means we're gonna go out again. We will. We will. Okay.

She reads the note again.

"Had to run." Maybe he jogs. Maybe he had a meeting and he didn't want to be late. Well, whatever—we'll figure it out when he calls. Plus, he forgot his tie. He forgot his tie—how cute is that? I'll return it to him when I see him. When he calls.

8.

We hear the sounds of an office—indistinct voices and phones ringing. She sits as though in a cubicle and wears a telephone headset. She is dressed in her "new look." She consults her laptop computer and dials a number.

Hello. Could I speak to Mr. Arnaby please?…How are you today, sir?…Oh, this is Mrs. Arnaby?…Oh, excuse me. Your voice sounded, uh…sorry. Is your husband available to come to the phone?…No? Well, could you please let him know that… my goodness. I didn't— …That's terrible. I'm awfully sorry… Yes, I'm sure it's extremely difficult… Well, perhaps I could help to ease your grief by offering you a special, three-month trial offer on our newest – …Hello? Hello?

She hangs up and slowly takes off her headset. She looks around nervously, and pulls the necktie from her pocket. She rubs it against her cheek, and smells it.

It's been three days. Three days. No phone call.

"Mapping out your Mate," says you should give him a three day grace period, and if he doesn't call by the third day, drop him like a hot potato.

In the grand scheme of things, three days isn't really that long. There could be lots of reasons why he hasn't called. Maybe he went out of town. Maybe he's been busy. He could be the type of person who needs a lot of space. And I wouldn't want to pressure him or seem really possessive or demanding.

Pause.

I just want to talk to him.

I bet that somewhere there's an article that says it's okay to call him. I didn't come across it. I probably didn't do enough research.

> *She takes a crumpled piece of paper from her pocket and stares at it for a moment. It has HIS phone number on it. Her phone rings, and she puts her headset back on.*

Good afternoon. Thank you for calling. How may I be of service... Oh, hello. Good afternoon, sir... No, I wasn't taking a break. The reason my line was open was, well...Yes, I'm just about finished my list...Yes, the A-R-N's will be done by the end of the day... Yes, I realize my daily sales are a bit low, but honestly not many people are interested today...What do you mean? ...No, I don't think it has anything to do with what I'm wearing... These are my normal clothes... I've changed my look a little bit... I thought I was still following dress code... Well, with all due respect, sir, I am on the telephone. No one actually sees— ...Okay, if you think it is inappropriate... Yes...I'm sorry... Okay... Good-bye.

> *She goes back to her call list and before she dials, she tries to pronounce the next name.*

...Mr. Arnazwick? ...Mr. Arnazwykee? ...Mr. Arnazahwickey?

> *She looks again at the crumpled piece of paper, looks around, looks at number.*

Oh fuck it.

> *She dials HIS number.*

...Oh, thank God. An answering machine...

Hi. Hello. It's me...from the other night. I just wanted to call and see how you're doing. I had a really nice time with you. We should do it again sometime. I'm free pretty much anytime. Tomorrow night, actually, there's a great movie playing at the library theatre. Or if that doesn't work, we could meet for coffee or lunch the next day. Just let me know when you're free. I have a car, so I could pick you up.

Pause.

I know I probably shouldn't say this, but I think about you a lot, and I think we got along really well. Oh, and I have your tie, in case you've been looking for it. It's a really nice tie, so you're probably wanting it back. So, call me. If you want. You have my number. Remember I wrote it on that napkin and you put it in your pocket. But just in case you lost it, my number is 423-67—...

The machine cut me off. Shit.

She stares at the phone for a moment, and then dials again.

It's busy. That's weird.

She hangs up and dials again.

Still busy. What the hell?

Maybe he just got home, and he didn't have a chance to check his messages because he had to make an important call. That must be it. That must be it. I'm sure he'll get my message. I'm sure he still has my number.

Pause. She looks around again, consults her call list and dials.

Hello. Could I speak to Mr. Arnazwickey please?... Oh, it's pronounced ehr-nah-swike? My apologies. How are you today, sir?

9.

The set is her living room. She stands centre stage wearing her sweater and pants over her red dress. She is out of breath and clutching a shopping bag.

Walking. I was walking…home…from work to clear my head. I was in a daze—going over and over everything in my head. Staring at the ground. Thinking about the first message, and then the second one, and the third one I left for him yesterday. Six days. I was thinking…

I looked up and there I was right in front of Ignite— by the big front window. My reflection—hair everywhere, glasses! I was wearing my glasses! I thought what am I doing here? What if HE's in there? What if he's in there looking for me? What if he's in there and he's hoping not to run into me? What if he's in there with someone else? What if this is a thing he does? What if—he sees me. Does he see me?

I want—but I can't. I can't. I back away running. I'm running home. Here where it's… Here. Here where maybe he called me back.

She takes off her sweater and hangs it on the mannequin.

Here where maybe he left me a message.

She goes to the phone and picks up the receiver.

No messages.

She wraps his number around the receiver and puts the receiver back on the phone. She goes to the mirror. Pause.

Oh! Jeez. I forgot. I bought him…

She takes an expensive men's sweater out of a

shopping bag. She stands in front of the mirror and holds it up.

A good size, I think.

She takes her sweater off the mannequin, and drapes the man's sweater on top. Pause. The phone rings. She stares at the phone for a few rings and picks up the receiver.

...Hello?...Oh. Hi...Good. I'm good... How are you?...Good... I—Did you—I guess you got my messages... Oh... That's okay. I've been pretty busy too... Yeah... So... (*Pause.*) Are you—? What?...Oh, yeah, okay, I'll hold...

She puts down the receiver and frantically looks through her magazines.

Shit! Where is it? "Post-Coital Phone Call— Answers for Awkward Phone Moments."

She skims the magazine article.

Ok...initiate...right...ask about...okay...open opportunities...right...gotcha...okay.

She puts the receiver to her ear. Long pause.

Hi!... Oh, no, no, no. That's okay. I know what it's like. Lots of calls... You must be a pretty busy guy, huh? ...Yeah, well, listen, do you, I mean, if you're free, I thought maybe you could come over tonight, and we could order Chinese food—there's this great movie on TV and...oh...oh...oh...okay...no, I understand...yup...okay...bye.

She hangs up the phone. Pause. She goes to the mirror. She looks like she might cry. She pulls the dress out of her pants. She looks angrily at the phone. She adjusts her breasts in the mirror.

Why didn't...

I don't…

I did—

What a…relief.

Pause.

I didn't really like him.

All he did was talk about himself.

And he spent the whole night staring at my boobs.

He didn't ask anything about me.

And he just left that morning—no goodbye.

This is…

She looks at the mannequin.

This is mine!

She takes the sweater off the mannequin and puts it on herself. She looks in the mirror. She looks at the couch, and pushes the magazines, and the shopping bag and the bag of chips on the floor. She sits on the couch. Pause. She looks at the phone and dials a number.

Hello?…I'd like to order some food for take-out… Um, some fried rice. One, no two egg rolls, and some chicken chow mein… Half an hour?… Great. Thank you.

She hangs up the phone. Pause. She picks up the remote and turns on the TV.

The End.

PACT

David Ferber

OCTOBER: I'm so freaked.

I've spent the last two weeks preparing myself for tonight…and it's not that I don't trust him, I do. I'm just…

He's so passionate about this whole thing, and I know he loves me—I love him too—but he can get kind of fanatical…

If I was totally at ease with all this, it wouldn't be so scary, right? Maybe my gut is telling me to just forget the whole thing. Like an instinctual fear…but I think about it, and who wouldn't be a little nervous, right? It's completely natural.

We really haven't known each other that long, but…I feel…at peace when it's just me and him…like nothing can hurt me. And maybe it's presumptuous of me to think that me and him…

I dunno, transcend this cliché of every other teenage couple…he's not like any other guy I've ever met, but…

…God, I'm scared.

Enter SAM, carrying a big duffel bag.

SAM: Hey, you're here.

OCTOBER: Of course I'm here. Why wouldn't I be?

SAM: Charlie said you might be a little late.

OCTOBER: I figured I'd just come straight here.

SAM: Are Sera an' Dana here?

OCTOBER: Naw, they went to grab some stuff at the Sev. The note on the door said to come down here and get comfy. What's in the bag?

SAM: Just some necessities of the evening.

OCTOBER: Alcohol. I'm flying dry tonight.

SAM: Naw, no booze. Just a few playful artifacts and such for some curious Asian rituals.

OCTOBER: "Rituals". It's so sick, Sam.

SAM: Well thanks, Smiley. So where's Charlie Boy?

OCTOBER: I don't know. He said he had to take care of some stuff and he'll be here around eleven-thirty.

            OCTOBER pulls a cigarette out of her jacket and lights it. SAM flops down on the couch. OCTOBER offers him a cigarette, which he refuses as he talks.

SAM: You'd think he'd be here half an hour early with a bottle of Jack rarin' to go. He loves shit like this.

OCTOBER: He is quite the weirdo.

SAM: I believe he prefers the term "eccentric". And don't get all superior, you're in on it too.

OCTOBER: Maybe, but my reasons aren't as fanatical as his.

SAM: Or mine, I suppose.

OCTOBER: Why are you here, Sam? I thought you wanted to keep to the texts and stay pure.

SAM: Well, Tobi, "To die without reaching one's aim is a dog's death, and fanaticism—but there is no shame in this."

OCTOBER: Hagakure?

SAM: Hagakure.

OCTOBER: I knew you couldn't go five minutes without quoting that stupid book.

SAM: It's my Way.

OCTOBER: Right.

OCTOBER addresses the audience.

I swear, he's the last guy you'd expect to be involved in something like this. Good at sports, popular. He's obsessed with Asian culture, and he's like…developed his own spirituality, based on all the old texts he's read. Most predominantly the Book of the Samurai, Hagakure. He's always talking about the Way. As if that'll keep him on the right track. Sam used to have a real dark side, but since he got into all this eastern discipline stuff, he's been a nice, sweet guy. Which is why it's so weird he's doing this. No one really knows his reasons except Charlie. I just know his plan is some Bushido ritual called "Seppuku".

OCTOBER watches as SAM pulls a large blade out of his duffel bag and starts to polish it.

…I need some fresh air.

SAM: *(Without looking up.)* Okay.

                OCTOBER leaves quickly and "Ain't Misbehavin"
                by Dinah Washington plays. The lights fade to black
                as the song stays for the lines "No one to talk with /
                all by myself / no one to walk with / but I'm happy on
                the shelf / ain't misbehavin' / I'm saving my love for
                you," as OCTOBER strolls out onto the porch,
                holding herself in the cold. She sits down as the song
                fades out, then addresses the audience as she smokes.

OCTOBER: I suppose you want an explanation. I'd like one
                myself. You'll understand.

                Enter DANA. She walks up to the steps.

DANA: Hey. Charlie and Sam here?

OCTOBER: Sam's downstairs, Charlie's gonna' be a little late.
                Where's Sera?

DANA: She's lagging behind.

OCTOBER: Where's the stuff from the Sev?

DANA: Sera's got it.

OCTOBER: She can barely walk and you're making her carry
                your groceries?

DANA: Sadistic, isn't it?

OCTOBER: Why are you playing with her like this?

DANA: It's an experiment in how cruel I can be, and how far
                you can push a fragile young body. Disgusting and
                lusty in a black widow sorta' way.

OCTOBER: Bye, Dana.

DANA: Yup.

                DANA goes inside, into her basement and stands
                behind the couch. She freezes with SAM, and
                OCTOBER continues.

OCTOBER: That's Dana Cleo. She's psychotic. I'm fuckin'
             serious. She makes Gary Oldman in *Dracula* look
             like Elmo from *Sesame Street*. I guess you could call
             her our leader. She set this whole thing up. Hand
             picked us one by one.

             *Enter SERA, very slowly, carrying two plastic bags
             and on the verge of collapse.*

SERA: Tobi, could you...

             *SERA drops the bags and wipes her forehead.
             OCTOBER throws away her cigarette, picks up the
             bags and drops them at the foot of the steps.*

             Thanks.

OCTOBER: Yeah, no problem.

SERA: Is Sam here yet?

OCTOBER: Yeah, he's downstairs. Are you okay?

             SERA starts climbing the steps to go inside.

SERA: Are you being sarcastic?

OCTOBER: This is so unhealthy, Sera.

             *SERA turns and puts a hand on OCTOBER's
             shoulder.*

SERA: Isn't that the point?

             Pause.

             I'll be inside.

OCTOBER: Yeah.

             *SERA follows DANA's suit, sits on the couch, and
             OCTOBER continues.*

             Dana had come up to me in the Caf that Monday,
             and told me she had been watching me, and she

wanted to help me. I told her to fuck off, and she says,

> *Lights come up on DANA.*

DANA: No, I don't want to stop you. I want to help you do it.

> *Lights on DANA go down.*

OCTOBER: I was intrigued. She told me she had this plan, and she was picking four kids to join her in a pact. I came to her house that Friday, two weeks ago.

> *OCTOBER comes into the basement, and the lights come up on the rest of them. They remain frozen as she talks.*

OCTOBER: You? What are you doing here?

SERA: The same thing you are.

OCTOBER: But you! You're a straight-A student, you're beautiful, you're...the most popular girl in school. You're rich...what the hell are you doing here?

SERA: Killing myself.

DANA: She's been doing it for a month already. Starving herself to death, and I'm the only one who noticed. Everyone's been like, "Oh, Sera! Are you losing weight? You look great!" And all this time...

SERA: Just shut up.

SAM: Leave her alone.

OCTOBER: But why? Your life is perfect!

SERA: I know. *(Pause)* ...It's such a bitch.

> *OCTOBER goes over to the table and chairs.*

OCTOBER: I couldn't believe it. Sera James! As if she could have anything in her life that's worthy of suicide.

After the fact…the pact, I mean, she came up to me in the cafeteria.

SERA gets up and goes over to the table.

SERA: Can I sit down?

OCTOBER: I suppose.

SERA sits.

SERA: You don't trust me, do you?

OCTOBER: What?

SERA: You think I'm bullshit, and I'm just doing this because…maybe daddy's not sending me to the university of my choice or something…you think you have real problems, and I just can't handle my paltry little rich girl problems, right?

OCTOBER: You could put it that way.

SERA: Why are you doing it?

OCTOBER: That's my business.

SERA: You can tell me.

OCTOBER: You said it yourself, Sera, I don't trust you.

SERA: You wanna' know why I am?

OCTOBER: I'd say I'm reasonably curious.

SERA: Don't you ever get the feeling that…your life has no direction? That the future is…so completely undesirable?

OCTOBER: Sera…you got into Harvard. Your perfect boyfriend Lee Miller had it broadcast over 97 for a week.

SERA: Exactly. Exactly. I'm going to Harvard to study law. …I want to be a painter.

OCTOBER: So why don't you?

SERA: I'm daddy's little girl.

                 I'm rich, yeah…but that means I have to be perfect
                 His version of perfect. I have to win all the beauty
                 pageants.

OCTOBER: And you do.

SERA: Yeah. I was on TV a lot. You know how the camera's
                 supposed to add ten pounds? My parents put me on
                 a scale every week to make sure I was ten pounds
                 underweight, so I'd look perfect. It didn't matter if I
                 was thirty pounds too thin, so long as I wasn't fat.

                 My friends are their friend's children. Even that
                 stuck up Lee Miller was hand-picked by my mother
                 If I get anything less than a 97 on anything they call
                 the school board and have it fixed.

                 My dad says "96 is the average of society's best. And
                 you are above that average."

                 And that's not going to happen now. I'll be thinner
                 than they ever could have imagined.

OCTOBER: Jesus.

SERA: Yeah. Dana was real impressed.

                 *OCTOBER gets up and starts strolling back to the
                 steps. SERA goes back to the couch.*

OCTOBER: So…she kinda' changed my mind about her. And
                 Dana was impressed. Sera's little patch on Dana's
                 tapestry will be about the inhumanity of
                 humanity—about how the impossible Hollywood
                 image of beauty is killing young women's spirits
                 She says it will also be a badge for parents to talk
                 with their kids instead of at them.

                 The only time I see any spark of goodness in Dana is
                 when she talks about the good impact our deaths
                 will have on society. She says people will wake up
                 and take notice…that we can really change things

Like some twisted fucking art form. A suicide tapestry.

She says it's got everything.

Sera; the innocent.

Sam; religion.

Charlie; the artist.

Me; poverty's bastard, and

Her; the only one who sees beauty in what we're doing. Well, Charlie does too, but Dana blows his appreciation for suicide right out of the water.

Speaking of Charlie...

She checks her watch.

Okay...here's the deal. I'm...I'm alive. Right now.

Of course I am. My point is, I...Two weeks ago, after a month and a half of consideration, I was ready to do it. If someone had handed me a bottle like this...

She pulls a bottle of pills out of her jacket pocket.

...I would have popped the cap and downed the whole thing. But then I met Charlie. And now...

OCTOBER goes back into the rec room.

I'd never even seen him before that Friday. I didn't know he existed. So...how was it exactly...Dana was standing like this. Uh...no...

She pushes DANA a foot to her left.

Right here. Sera was there, Sam was there, and I was right in the middle.

She hops over the couch and sits in the middle.

So we're sitting here talking...insignificant stuff...

DANA: So…Sammy Boy. How're you going to do it? Pop some pills?

SAM: No. It's a ritualistic suicide.

DANA: Perfect! Even better! What, do you drink poison and chant a mantra or something?

SAM: I gut myself.

OCTOBER: Y'know, the usual suicide pact small talk. And then I say,

             "So who are we waiting for anyway?"

             Then the doorbell rings and the lights go out.

             I know, I know. It looks totally clichè, but that's what actually happened.

DANA: Shit, something must have tripped the breaker. Hold on…

             DANA gets up and leaves. Enter CHARLIE. The lights come up.

             (*Offstage.*) Are they on?

CHARLIE: Yeah.

             Enter DANA.

DANA: Ah. Good. Everyone, this is Charlie Duncan.

OCTOBER
& SAM: Hey.

SERA: Charlie?

CHARLIE: Hey, Sera.

SERA: Charlie, what are you—

CHARLIE: Are we all really going to do this, or is this just a get-to-know-you thing?

DANA: We're doing it. I suppose you want formalities.

CHARLIE: Introductions would be nice, yeah. Just because we're all killing ourselves doesn't mean we can't be civil about it.

DANA: Alright. This hunk of flesh is the ever-popular Sam Benjamin, who I'm sure you know of, and…I think you know Sera.

CHARLIE: I do.

DANA: The quiet one in the middle is October Salenger.

             CHARLIE and OCTOBER make eye contact, and OCTOBER jumps off the couch.

OCTOBER: Okay, y'see? Y'see that? Did you catch this eye contact we just had here? What was that? Y'know what that was?

             Recognition.

             She sits back on the couch and returns her gaze to CHARLIE.

CHARLIE: Well hello, October.

OCTOBER: Hi.

CHARLIE: Out of curiosity, why are you in on this whole thing?

DANA: Dad beats her, stepbrother tried to rape her. She's got other shit going on, too, but she hasn't really told me much.

OCTOBER: Could you believe she'd just out and say that? I couldn't believe she did that.

SERA: Can we just do this?

CHARLIE: Fine, let's go.

             OCTOBER gets off the couch and strolls over to the table as the lights go down on the Rec Room and come up on the table. Exit all but her.

OCTOBER: The thing that really impressed me was the fact that he was able to keep his sense of humor in such a...morbid situation. But I'm not about to fall all over a guy just because he keeps his cool, especially one I meet at a suicide pact.

But I felt something for him...just in his eyes. It was a connection. You know when you feel that? When, like...you're on the bus, and you make eye contact with just...some person, and you don't even know their name, but you can't really forget them? It was like that.

So anyway, the way the pact worked was that we lived for another two weeks, tied up all the loose ends in our lives, and came to Dana's tonight to...commence the pact. We're not gonna' all drink some purple brew and sleep or nothin'. It's not like a cult. Dana knows her shit about suicide if nothing else, and she knows it's a very personal thing.

OCTOBER counts on her fingers.

Charlie's supposed to slit his wrists. At first he wanted to blow his brains out, but he decided that if he slit his wrists, not only would that make it easier to have an open casket, but he didn't think it would make such a violent transition into death. He likes the idea of watching his life squirt out through his wrists. Sam's gonna' do that "Seppuku" thing. Sera said if she wasn't dead by tonight, she'd slit her wrists like all those models did in the late eighties. I'm supposed to pop a month's supply of valium, and Dana's going to hang herself over all our bodies, once they've been arranged in her room.

Her parents are due back tomorrow at six in the morning. Dana says the plan is we all get together tonight, compose our notes—she insists on notes—and we all have to be dead by five. She wants the bodies to be as fresh as possible when her parents find us, so the shock will be from the sight and not the smell. She wants them to be traumatized for life.

Dana has issues.

OCTOBER sits down at the table.

So anyway, Charlie was in the back of my mind for the next two days, but I didn't go looking for him. He found me in the library at school. I was sitting there with a book of Poe, and in he walks.

Enter CHARLIE. OCTOBER doesn't notice.

CHARLIE: You like Poe?

OCTOBER: What?

CHARLIE: Edgar Allan Poe. You into that old type of horror?

OCTOBER: I just like the poetry.

CHARLIE: "Come read to me some poem, some simple heartfelt lay, that shall soothe this restless feeling, and banish thoughts of day."

OCTOBER: That's beautiful. Poe?

CHARLIE sits.

CHARLIE: Longfellow.

OCTOBER: Would you like to sit down?

CHARLIE: I would.

             So what's new?

OCTOBER: Well, I'm in a suicide pact.

CHARLIE: Yeah, why?

OCTOBER: Why what?

CHARLIE: Why are you doing this?

OCTOBER: Were you not listening when Dana told you the other day? I've got some shit going on.

CHARLIE: Yeah, but it's kind of a cheap way out of your
             problems, isn't it?

             Pause.

OCTOBER: You swore in, too.

CHARLIE: What's your point?

OCTOBER: Aren't you being just a little hypocritical?

CHARLIE: I don't have any problems to escape from. I just
             think the world sucks, so I'm getting out of it. It just
             sucks. Wherever you go there are assholes, and
             wherever you go there are murderers. Taxes, ugly
             teachers, bad plumbing, bathrooms with no toilet
             paper, shit like that. It's not life that sucks, it's just
             the world.

OCTOBER: The Earth sucks, so you're leaving.

             *CHARLIE lights a cigarette, takes a puff and hands
             it to OCTOBER.*

CHARLIE: Yup.

OCTOBER: That's it.

CHARLIE: Basically.

             OCTOBER takes a puff and hands it back.

OCTOBER: You're nuts.

CHARLIE: Maybe we're all a little crazy. But, lovers and
             madmen have such seething brains. Such shaping
             fantasies, that apprehend more than cool reason
             ever comprehends.

OCTOBER: Midsummer Night's Dream.

CHARLIE: Very good.

             Cool moment of silence.

OCTOBER: Wanna' fuck?

Pause.

CHARLIE: Did you just say what I think you said?

OCTOBER: What do you think I said?

CHARLIE: I think you just said 'wanna fuck?'

OCTOBER: Then yes.

CHARLIE: That's your philosophy on sex? No courting, no romance. Just 'wanna fuck?'

OCTOBER: Not usually, but maybe I'm willing to make the leap with you.

CHARLIE: Maybe you just need a shrink.

OCTOBER: Oh really? And what would he say?

CHARLIE: 'Young, screwed-up codependant girl with fucked-up home life and abusive father who needs to throw herself at boys and give up her charms in order to gratify some kind of male/slash/female inferiority issues'.

OCTOBER: Uh-huh. What's with the psychobabble?

CHARLIE: Grew up in foster homes. In the ones where the fathers weren't tryin' to bugger me the people would be like, new-age hippies. 'Peace, man. Gratification of the soul pleases the body, dude.' Shit like that. I know my psychobabble.

OCTOBER: Foster homes.

CHARLIE: Yup.

OCTOBER: The guys would try to fuck you.

CHARLIE: Some.

OCTOBER: And I thought my life was screwed up. Gimmie.

             CHARLIE hands the cigarette back.

CHARLIE: Everybody's life's got static, Tobi. You cry for me, I feel bad for you. And if that's not happening we feel sorry for ourselves. It's a fucked-up world.

OCTOBER: And that's why you're leaving.

CHARLIE: Among other things.

OCTOBER: Like what?

CHARLIE: Personal shit.

OCTOBER: Nothing you'll tell me, I suppose?

CHARLIE: That's right.

                Another silence begins.

                They both seem fairly comfortable with it.

                Silence ends.

OCTOBER: So you wanna' fuck?

                CHARLIE stands.

CHARLIE: I think I'll go hang around some sane people for a little change of pace.

OCTOBER: What, are you gay? Am I like, ugly, or something?

CHARLIE: You're beautiful. And I'm one hundred percent straight, but 'fucking' you was never on my list of priorities.

                CHARLIE raises her wrist and kisses it.

                ...I'll see you around.

                Exit CHARLIE.

OCTOBER: Whoah.

                OCTOBER gets up and starts to go over to the steps.

                This thoroughly impressed me.

She sits down.

I can't explain why exactly. I...I've never really fallen in love before. I've had a few really intense crushes, but love...just never happened for me. Guys are pricks, for the most part. Really, think about it. How many guys do you know that...count this out, now, are...

She counts on her fingers.

...mature, poetic, romantic, honourable, well-read and erotic before sexy? I've been on this planet seventeen shitty years and he's the first one I've met. And now...

Okay, he does have his bad qualities;

Counts on her fingers.

His lust for life can go to extremes. He can get a little fanatical. He should be dead by the end of the night, and he's always fucking late.

Enter SERA onto the steps.

SERA: Haven't you gotten enough air yet?

OCTOBER: What?

SERA: Sam said you came out here for air. Have you breathed enough?

OCTOBER: I'm waiting for Charlie.

SERA: Oh. I figured. Have you noticed anything weird about Sam?

OCTOBER: Aside from the plan to gut himself? No.

SERA: He's been looking at me funny.

OCTOBER: He's probably just upset to see you starving yourself like you are. Sam's sweet like that.

SERA: No...it's not that.

OCTOBER: Well funny like how?

SERA: Funny like... Lust.

OCTOBER: Oh...that's not too funny.

SERA: It's creepy. I mean, this is Sam! And it's not so much that it's Sam, it's just that look...that's all it is...lust. There's no love. No warmth. You know what Sam was like in grade school?

OCTOBER: I've heard stories.

SERA: Stories like what?

OCTOBER: He had problems. Violence problems.

SERA: He was the bully. But it wasn't just that he was the bully. He loved being the bully. It...gave him some kind of sick pleasure to see other kids break. I mean, if he hadn't gotten the help and discipline that he did...I'd be scared just going to school with him.

OCTOBER: He got help.

SERA: His parents put him in a self-defense class, so he'd combine his strength with the discipline in how to use it. Sam liked what he found. Now he knows enough to write a doctorate on eastern religions.

             I remember...once. Once he broke Tyler Graham. He beat him right into the ground. His fists were like...dripping blood. And I remember watching him standing over Tyler, and he had this look of...

OCTOBER: Lust?

SERA: Yeah, but...violent at the same time. And now the way he looks at me...it scares me. He's not like Charlie. Charlie's violence is channeled into his writing and poetry. But Sam's is...bottled. When Charlie looks at you with passion...it warms you, too. It makes you feel the same way. Sam's way just makes me shiver.

OCTOBER: How long ago was it?

SERA: What, the Tyler Graham thing?

OCTOBER: You and Charlie.

SERA: Two years ago.

OCTOBER: What was he like?

SERA: He was like…how he is now. But less disciplined. He was a boy. Now he's a man. And you've got him…and you know exactly what I mean when I tell you how he can look at you.

OCTOBER: What happened with you two? I get this vibe that the pair of you didn't really want to part ways.

SERA: We don't have to talk about this.

OCTOBER: It doesn't bother me.

SERA: Okay…I don't want to talk about it.

OCTOBER: You guys…You kind of have this…

SERA: Understanding.

OCTOBER: Yeah. And you know.

SERA: Know what?

OCTOBER: Why…. he's so…romantic about everything. About a sunset, about a situation, about life.

            Everything. He loves music and poetry and sex and drama and dreams and madness…he loves it. He gives me this bullshit thing about wanting to experience it… He says, "death is the greatest kick of all—that's why they saved it for last".

            And it's bullshit. I know it is.

Pause.

…what?

SERA: He didn't tell you anything?

OCTOBER: Get serious! He never shuts up with all these theories on life and love and… But you can tell. It's all bullshit. It's like…empty.

SERA: That's Charlie.

OCTOBER: Yeah, that's Charlie.

SERA: You didn't know him at all when he was younger…did you?

OCTOBER: I'd never met him before…

SERA: He was different. He was…he was like Sam. This romance thing he uses like a religion…none of that existed before… He was an asshole, he really was. And he was getting worse and worse. Fighting, stealing cars. Drugs and drinking all the time. He was…he was this total hellspawn.

                And then one summer, between grade ten and eleven, he just disappeared.

OCTOBER: What happened?

SERA: I have no clue. But after that summer he came back to school—two weeks late—like a whole new person. He was all smiles and poetry… Crazy shit. We thought he'd lost his mind, but…He was a cooler guy.

OCTOBER: And he never told you what happened?

SERA: Nope. But knowing the way he was before… Something must have just fucked his reality right up. And the reason this suicide crap doesn't fit with him is because it doesn't fit with him now. It fits with him then.

The reason it sounds like bullshit is because it's bullshit.

Where is he? It's midnight already.

OCTOBER: He said he'd be late.

SERA stands and picks up the bags.

SERA: Yeah, but this is extreme.

OCTOBER: You seem a little more chipper. Did you eat something?

SERA: Dana gave me a dose of caffeine pills.

OCTOBER: Won't that burn out any energy you have left?

SERA: I think that's her plan.

OCTOBER: Oh.

SERA: Well, I just came out for the Haagen Dazs. Don't want it to melt. I'll see you in a bit, okay?

OCTOBER: Okay. Bye Sera.

Exit SERA.

She's a sweetheart. Once I got to know her better I liked her a lot more than before. I can still do without that Dana freak, though.

Oh…I guess I've told you about everyone but me, right?

Uh…here's the rundown; My name is October Salenger. I know it's a weird name, my mother was a hippie. I'm seventeen and I'm in grade twelve at Westwood Collegiate. The prom…

She checks her watch.

…ended four minutes ago. I was there with Charlie for about an hour and a half and left at eleven fifteen to come here. We made the pact two weeks ago today, so…tonight's the night.

Why am I doing this…I…My reasons were this;

My parents split up when I was five. For some reason my drunk father got custody instead of my rich mother. I'm an only child, or was until my dad got remarried to Queen Bitch, who brought her date-raping son along for the ride.

My dad is really abusive. Like physically abusive. And my stepbrother tried to rape me twice. Maybe…maybe those aren't the reasons, maybe those are just the triggers.

I dunno. I just felt like my life didn't…I felt like I wasn't…it sounds clichè, but I felt like I wasn't…like me, like life wasn't worth the six pack of beer it took to bring me into it. …and now…

She checks her watch again and stands.

It's like ten after twelve. Where is he?

She waits a moment and checks her watch again.

Fuck it. I'm goin' to get my smokes.

"'S Wonderful" by Sarah Vaughan plays. OCTOBER goes into the house, and the lights go down. Music stays for the lines "'S wonderful / 's marvelous / you should care for me / 's awful nice / 's paradise / 's what I love to see" and the lights come up on OCTOBER sitting in the middle of the couch, with SAM on one side and SERA on the other. SAM and SERA are writing, and OCTOBER has a pad of paper on her lap.

SAM: Okay, check this out;

                  "Anyone who really knows me understands my reasons, though they may not respect them. This is my way. This is The Way." Signed, Sam J. Kilmer.

OCTOBER: Very poetic, Sam.

SAM: Are you being facetious?

OCTOBER: I was trying to be sarcastic.

SERA: Well, isn't that what facetious means?

OCTOBER: No, facetious is nicer. How's yours?

SERA: I can't do it, I can't think straight. When my mind isn't racing from those damn pills it feels like my head's full of cotton balls.

OCTOBER: Want some help?

SERA: No, I'm okay. Maybe I just need a rest. Daaaaana!

DANA: (Offstage.) What?

SERA: Come in here!

               Enter DANA from her room, carrying a noose.

DANA: What? I'm kinda' in the middle of something here.

SERA: Do I have to write this now? I need to lie down for a bit.

DANA: You think you'll die?

SERA: I don't know, I just want to sleep. Be patient, okay?

DANA: Fine, have a snooze. Excuse *me* for being excited.

               Exit DANA back into her room. SERA curls up on the end of the couch and deposits her head in OCTOBER's lap.

OCTOBER: That girl is demented.

SERA: Mmm hmm. Do you mind if I lie like this?

OCTOBER: No, I'm fine.

SERA: Thanks.

Enter CHARLIE, carrying a backpack.

OCTOBER: Where the hell were you?

SERA: Charlie.

CHARLIE: Just takin' care of some stuff.

SERA: Hi.

SAM: Taking care of what, exactly?

CHARLIE: Personal shit.

SAM: *(Grumbling.)* It's always personal fucking shit with you.

OCTOBER: Seriously, where were you?

CHARLIE: Just out walkin'. Thinkin'.

OCTOBER: 'Till one forty-five? About what?

              Enter DANA.

DANA: Charlie! Good. C'mere, I need to talk to you.

CHARLIE: Yeah.

              CHARLIE and DANA go toward her room.

OCTOBER: Hey.

DANA: What?

OCTOBER: Not you, him.

              CHARLIE comes back to the couch, and OCTOBER leans her head back.

OCTOBER: C'mere.

              CHARLIE stands over her.

Closer.

              CHARLIE leans in.

Closer.

> *CHARLIE leans in further. OCTOBER reaches up, pulls her to him and kisses him, then pushes him away.*

Now go away.

CHARLIE: Yes ma'am.

DANA: Come along, Edgar Allan.

> *Exit CHARLIE and DANA.*

OCTOBER: What were we talking about?

SAM: You said my note sucked.

OCTOBER: No, after that.

SAM: I dunno. You think mine is so bland, why don't you read me yours?

OCTOBER: I'm not writing one.

SAM: But Dana said—

OCTOBER: As if you or I really give a shit about Dana. I don't need a note. Dana'll go along with it. She'll probably think not leaving a note reflects the tragedy of my life and thusly my death.

SAM: Jesus, you think you're so smart.

OCTOBER: What is with you lately?

SAM: What?

OCTOBER: You've been acting like a total ass all night.

SAM: Excuse me?

OCTOBER: You're, like, picking on everyone. What's with you?

SAM: Nothing.

OCTOBER: Sera, back me up here.

SERA doesn't move.

Sera. C'mon, is he being a jerk or is it just me? Sera? Oh Jesus, is she dead?

SAM: She's just asleep, you ditz.

OCTOBER: Y'see? Y'see? Shit like that. That's what I'm talking about. You've never said shit like that before.

SAM: Oh, whatever. Look, she's breathing. You can tell. She just must be passed out. Sera, honey. C'mon.

SAM gives SERA a light smack on the cheek.

OCTOBER: Hey!

OCTOBER hits SAM hard on the shoulder.

You prick! She's weak enough as it is! Are you paying attention to yourself here? You're acting like a total dick! Have you been drinking?

SAM: No!

OCTOBER: Well what the hell, then? You're insulting me, you're hitting Sera—

SAM: I didn't hit her!

OCTOBER: What was that?

SAM: A light smack to wake her up!

OCTOBER: That was a hit!

SAM jumps off the couch.

SAM: Shut up, alright! I never hit her!

OCTOBER: Are you, like, pulling away from your disciplines here because it's the last night? Is that what this is?

SAM: What? No. I…Am I really that different?

OCTOBER: You hit her!

SAM: I didn't fucking—

            SAM goes to slug OCTOBER, but stops and pulls his fist back. OCTOBER just stares at him as DANA and CHARLIE enter.

CHARLIE: Okay, what'd we miss?

            Exit SAM.

            What was that?

OCTOBER: He's been acting like a jerk all night. I have no idea what his problem is, he just freaked out.

CHARLIE: I'll go talk to him.

OCTOBER: No, you stay here, let Dana go.

SERA: I'll go.

OCTOBER: Hey, you're awake.

SERA: I was asleep?

OCTOBER: Sam hit you and it didn't wake you up.

DANA: You must have just passed out again.

OCTOBER: Again?

            SERA stands and starts to go after SAM.

SERA: It happens… I'll go after Sam. Hi Charlie.

CHARLIE: Hey Sera. Dana, company.

            Exit SERA.

DANA: What?

CHARLIE: Give Sera some company. But let her handle Sam.

DANA: What, you don't think I have the human touch?

OCTOBER: Of an embalmer, maybe.

DANA gives OCTOBER the finger, and leaves after SERA.

C'mere. I need a hug.

CHARLIE hops onto the couch, and OCTOBER curls up against him.

So what did you think about when you were out walking?

CHARLIE: Stuff.

OCTOBER: Quit it. What stuff?

CHARLIE: The stuff like the other night.

OCTOBER: Yeah...it was pretty good, wasn't it?

CHARLIE: No, I mean what we talked about.

OCTOBER: Oh. You still...

CHARLIE: I'm unconvinced.

OCTOBER: ...Charlie...

Okay, time out.

OCTOBER gets off the couch and addresses the audience.

What he's talking about is a conversation we had last Saturday. We were at...I think it was a Perkins or something...maybe an Earl's...I dunno', it wasn't a coffee shop, it was a restaurant.

She and CHARLIE go and sit at the table.

The conversation had taken several twists and turns, and then it came to this;

"Well...I'm kind of having second thoughts."

CHARLIE: You can't be serious!

OCTOBER: Why not? A week ago I was a wreck! But then you showed up and I'm beginning to...

CHARLIE: To look at things in a whole new way, I suppose? Don't feel suicidal any more?

OCTOBER: Well, yeah.

CHARLIE: That's just bullshit, Tobi, it really is. This is a fuckin' pact. We all swore to do it after the prom. You don't just up and say 'Oops, wait a minute, I'm starting to have a good time here, guys. Maybe I don't really want to do this.' I mean, suicide is a cheap-ass way out of your problems, but being cheap-ass about suicide, well...you just can't get more cheap-ass than that!

OCTOBER: That's not even close to being funny.

CHARLIE: Every one of us has sat down and completely figured suicide is the way out. We figured this out weeks, probably years before we made the pact. This wasn't some "oh my God, I just can't take this any more, I'm gonna' kill myself" thing. Your problems aren't just going to go away, October. They'll be waiting for you after the prom.

OCTOBER: What if you don't kill yourself?

CHARLIE: Don't even try this, I'm doing it, with or without you. This is something that goes far beyond you and I bein' together.

OCTOBER: Charlie, I really care for you. I'd kill for you. But I don't think I'm ready to die for you.

CHARLIE: Well I'd die for you, baby, but I'm not willing to live for ya'.

OCTOBER gets up and goes back to the couch. CHARLIE follows.

OCTOBER: What can I say to make you understand?

CHARLIE: Y'see...what the thing is is...slitting my wrists has nothing to do with any problems I'm trying to escape from.

I know I'm young, and I know there's billions more experiences out there waiting for me, but...The only one I really look forward to is losing this...flesh. Crossing over to a whole new type of existence. Learning what the point of this one really is.

Pause.

OCTOBER: Bullshit.

CHARLIE: Pardon?

OCTOBER: Bullshit. Sera told me about your personal renaissance.

CHARLIE: What does that have to do with anything?

OCTOBER: What were you like before?

CHARLIE: Sera doesn't know shit, Tobi.

OCTOBER: Tell me the truth.

CHARLIE: Why would I lie?

OCTOBER: Because maybe you're ashamed. Maybe who you are now doesn't like who you were then. Maybe deep down inside you're still the same person. Maybe you're scared, too.

CHARLIE: ...maybe you're grasping at straws.

OCTOBER: Doesn't the idea...of experiencing life...with me...inspire you to stay just a little?

Pause.

Charlie?

Enter DANA, SAM and SERA.

DANA: Alright everybody! Notes!

OCTOBER: Sam, are you okay?

SAM: *(Aloof.)* Yeah, I'm fine. Gimmie a pen.

OCTOBER: No, you're note's good. It's…to the point.

SAM: You really think so?

OCTOBER: Well…yeah.

                 DANA picks up a pad of paper on the coffee table.

DANA: Sera, what is this?

SERA: That's for Charlie.

DANA: You want to be stripped naked after you're dead?

SERA: And put in a black satin sheet. I brought one in my bag…

DANA: You want to be stripped naked, and put in a black satin sheet.

SERA: Yeah…it'll be to show my parents how thin I've become. That's what they wanted.

SAM: Whoah, are you gettin' a mean hard-on or is that just me?

SERA: Sam, don't do that.

SAM: What?

SERA: Just don't…don't talk about me like that. Okay? Please?

SAM: Ah, whatever. Charlie, c'mere.

                 SAM starts rifling through his duffle bag.

                 You ready to run the drill?

CHARLIE: "The Drill"?

SAM: Yeah. You're my kaishaku.

OCTOBER: Kaiwhatwho?

SAM: Kaishaku. The assistant in seppuku.

CHARLIE: Assistant in what?

OCTOBER: What, you don't know?

CHARLIE: Don't know what?

OCTOBER: You never told him?

CHARLIE: What the funny fuck!

SAM pulls one short (Wakizashi) and one long (Katana) samurai sword out of his duffle bag.

SAM: Uh...okay buddy, let me explain this...

SAM and CHARLIE get up and walk off to beside the couch. DANA and SERA sit down.

This one's for me, this one's for you.

SAM hands CHARLIE the long blade.

DANA: What's this?

OCTOBER: Oh, you're gonna love it.

CHARLIE: Can someone tell me what the fuck is going on?

SAM: Well...it's my suicide. It's assisted. I want you to, y'know, make the fatal stroke.

CHARLIE: Then how is that a suicide? That just means I kill you. That's not suicide, that's me killing you.

SAM: Could you just listen?

CHARLIE: Fine.

SAM: Here, hold this. Get a feel for it. Now in seppuku...

OCTOBER: That's the name of the ritual.

SAM: Can I explain this, please?

OCTOBER: Sorry.

SAM: In seppuku, I kneel on the ground, with my back to you.

            SAM kneels in front of CHARLIE, with his back to him.

CHARLIE: Why?

SAM: It'd take too long to explain why, can you just let me explain how?

CHARLIE: Yeah, fine.

SAM: Okay, now what happens is I take this blade and cut open my stomach, spilling my intestines.

CHARLIE: Won't that kill you by itself?

SAM: That's not the *ritual*, asshole, it has to be done *right!* Now are you going to listen or do I have to recruit Dana?

            DANA perks at the idea.

CHARLIE: No, no, I'll be your kaiwhatwho.

SAM: Kaishaku. I cut open my stomach, spill my intestines, and just experience the pain for a count of ten.

CHARLIE: Is that in the ritual?

SAM: Well…actually, no. I just wanted to see how much it would hurt to get my bowels ripped out.

OCTOBER: That's sarcasm.

SAM: No, I'm actually kinda' curious just how much it really could hurt. I mean, how much pain is possible?

OCTOBER: Ew. A lot, I'm sure.

CHARLIE: Okay, so you gut yourself, and then?

SAM: You chop my head off.

CHARLIE: Excuse me, I what?

SAM: You decapitate me.

CHARLIE: I'm not cutting your head off, forget it!

              SAM stands.

SAM: It's a great honour to be chosen as kaishaku.

CHARLIE: Well honour Dana!

SAM: You're my only friend here, Charlie!

CHARLIE: Y'know what? I never really liked you.

SAM: Charlie, c'mon.

OCTOBER: You talked about new experiences...this would certainly rank.

              Pause.

SAM: Come on, Charlie...you're the only one I trust.

              Pause. CHARLIE looks at his long sword.

CHARLIE: ...oh, you had better be *so* thankful for this.

              CHARLIE gives SAM his sword.

SAM: *Yes!!!* I knew I could count on you!

CHARLIE: Ah, shut up. I'm goin' out for a smoke.

DANA: You can smoke down here.

CHARLIE: I'm going *outside*. For a *smoke*. *Out*side. Any problems?

              Everyone shakes their heads.

CHARLIE: Okay.

SAM: I knew I could count on you.

CHARLIE: Fuck you!

                Exit CHARLIE.

SAM: I don't think he appreciates what an honour this is.

                SERA stands.

SERA: Tobi, can I borrow your coat?

OCTOBER: Yeah, sure.

                SERA puts on OCTOBER's coat and goes for the door.

                Where are you going?

SERA: Just upstairs.

OCTOBER: In my coat.

SERA: I'll be right back.

                Exit SERA. There's an uncomfortable pause.

DANA: So Tobi. How's your note coming?

OCTOBER: I didn't write one. The way I figure, the only person who gives a shit about me is dying tonight, so I don't really need one. Like you said, I'm poverty's bastard, right?

                Another uncomfortable pause. "A Sinner Kissed An Angel" by Freddy Cole comes up.

DANA: Right.

                The lights fade out, leaving it dark for the lines "stars in the sky were dancing / the night was perfect for romancing / the night a sinner kissed an angel", and comes up on CHARLIE on the steps, smoking.

                Enter SERA.

SERA: Hey sexy.

CHARLIE: *(Without turning around.)* I can't believe he wants me
               to chop off his fucking head.

               SERA sits down beside him.

SERA: You okay?

CHARLIE: As well as can be expected. Can you believe him?

SERA: You're not upset about that, you're worried about
               Tobi.

CHARLIE: Aw, don't get psychological on me, Sera—

SERA: She wants to bail on the pact, and you're scared
               about it.

CHARLIE: How d'you figure all that?

SERA: I know you. And she's pretty easy to read. To me,
               anyway.

               Pause.

CHARLIE: Sam's got you pretty freaked.

SERA: He's...loosing his demons. All the discipline's
               falling away, and...

CHARLIE: Well, don't worry. He'll be dead before me, and I'll
               make sure he keeps his hands off you.

SERA: Dead or alive?

CHARLIE: What?

SERA: You saw his reaction. He...he wants to...dead or
               alive.

CHARLIE: Come on! Sam's actin' a little off tonight, but he's no
               necrophile.

SERA: Just tell me you'll keep him away from me.

CHARLIE: Alright, I'll keep him away from you.

SERA: And tell me you'll protect October.

CHARLIE: Protect her?

SERA: From Dana. She'll force her when October tries to quit the pact.

CHARLIE: Yeah.

SERA: And she wants you to stay with her. To live.

CHARLIE: Yes she does.

SERA: And will you?

CHARLIE: Haven't decided.

SERA: But will you do that? Watch for us, I mean. Dana's out of her mind, and Sam's losing his, I can feel it. But he…he's right to trust you…you're the only one I do.

They look at each other.

CHARLIE: Sera, why are you looking at me like that?

SERA: Do you ever wish things had been different?

CHARLIE: For you. For Tobi. I wish you guys had had it easier.

SERA: I mean between us.

CHARLIE: Like you and me?

SERA: Yeah.

CHARLIE: I'm with October.

SERA: And me?

CHARLIE: We don't need to talk about this.

SERA: I do. I need to hear it.

CHARLIE: Hear what?

SERA: I need to hear that…someone…someone outside my parent's little chic clique…do you still have any affection for me? Anything at all?

CHARLIE: Sera…

SERA: Kiss me.

CHARLIE: No.

SERA: October loves you. She needs you, too. Like me. Say it. I need to hear it. I'm dying, Charlie. Even if I went straight to a hospital, those fucking speeds Dana gave me… I'm dying.

               Say it.

CHARLIE: I love you.

SERA: Say it again.

CHARLIE: I love you, Sera.

SERA: Could you do me one more favour?

CHARLIE: Yeah.

SERA: Hold still.

               SERA kisses him softly.

               Thanks.

CHARLIE: Oh, that man might know the end of this day's business ere it come.

SERA: What's that from?

CHARLIE: Julius Caesar.

               Enter OCTOBER. She stands for a moment just watching them before SERA notices her.

SERA: Hey.

OCTOBER: Hey. Are you okay?

CHARLIE: I'm always okay.

OCTOBER: I'm serious.

CHARLIE: S'well as can be expected.

OCTOBER: Well...we'll be inside.

CHARLIE: Yeah.

> *"Lost Mind" by Diana Krall comes up. Stays for the lines "if you could be so kind / to help me find my mind / I'd like to thank you in advance" as the lights fade.*
>
> *The lights come up on the rec room, DANA and SAM are on the couch.*

DANA: So where do you suppose you'll go, Sammy?

SAM: What do you mean?

DANA: I mean up or down. Heaven or Hell.

SAM: I never thought about it.

DANA: What? A psycho Bhuddist Bushido freak like you?

SAM: I'm not a Bhuddist.

DANA: Close enough.

SAM: I kinda' figure it is whatever it is, and I'll find out soon enough.

DANA: Unless the Christians were right.

SAM: Yeah, yeah, I know. Stuck in Limbo.

             ...Where'd they all go? It's been forever.

DANA: Oh, let the losers do what they want. You're not uncomfortable just you and me, are you?

SAM: Uh, no... It's just...y'know, Charlie. A man needs other men. Especially in a suicide pact.

DANA: At least we girls bring some intelligence and integrity to this whole suicide thing. You guys are doing it for shit reasons.

SAM: As if! October and Sera are doing it to escape their shitty lives, and Christ, Dana, you're just doing it for kicks! I have my reasons!

DANA: Yeah, yeah. "The Way of the Warrior is found in death." Very honourable.

SAM: You wouldn't undertsand.

DANA: Oh, yes, of course not. Unlike men, who off themselves when their car gets a scratch, women, through whom suicide has become a more refined practice, wouldn't understand your reasons.

              Enter SERA and OCTOBER.

SAM: Excuse me, women better suicide?

DANA: Of course.

              SERA sits at the end of the couch, OCTOBER in the chair.

SAM: Oh please! Men *know* suicide. Girls try to kill themselves on a whim! For guys, it's an actual, conscious decision.

              Men think it out more, plan it better, and pull it off. For girls it's just a death-defying cry for help! Guys know no one gives a shit, and that's why they go for the gusto!

OCTOBER: Shut up, Sam.

SAM: But I'm right!

SERA: She's right, shut up! …just…be quiet…

              SERA curls up on the end of the couch and closes her eyes.

SAM: You know I'm right. Tell her I'm right!

DANA: The only point you're making is that girls know how to manipulate people better than men.

SAM: No! No, fuck you. Girls just don't take suicide seriously.

OCTOBER: Nonono! Look at us. Here we are, five kids completely committed to a self-inflicted end, and sixty percent of us are girls. We know what we're doing, and here we are. Argue that.

SAM: We're a bunch of freaks! I'm not saying you or Dana or Sera aren't committed to this, but the general populous of women are spineless when it comes to suicide. Y'see that? The man knows. Eat that, Sera!

            SAM gives SERA a light smack in the arm. She doesn't move.

            Sera. Sera, honey, you gotta' eat more or you're not gonna' have the strength to die.

            SAM gives her a little shake.

            Fuckin' passed out again.

DANA: I'll get her a blanket.

            DANA gets up and leaves, and OCTOBER goes over to SERA. Enter CHARLIE.

SAM: Go get her something to eat.

OCTOBER: She won't eat anything.

SAM: She's usually not this hard to wake up.

OCTOBER: Sera!

CHARLIE: Check for a pulse.

SAM: Oh, there you are, man! Hey, who do you think takes suicide more seriously, men or women?

CHARLIE: What? Check for a pulse, Tobi.

OCTOBER: Okay. *(She checks.)*

SAM: Her pulse is just fine. Don't you go changing the subject!

            OCTOBER stands quickly.

OCTOBER: No it's not. I need some...I need some fresh air.

            OCTOBER grabs her coat off the chair.

CHARLIE: Aw, Christ, Sera. ...Aw, Christ, Sera...

            CHARLIE holds SERA's body. OCTOBER kisses him on the cheek, hugs him and leaves.

SAM: Well, that's that. Come on, let's drag her into Dana's room.

CHARLIE: ...this isn't right. This isn't even close to being right...what the fuck...aw, Sera...

            SAM goes to take a hold of SERA's arm to drag her into DANA's room. CHARLIE smacks his hand away.

            Don't touch her!

SAM: Jesus, what's your problem?

            Don't start waxing sentimental, Charlie. This is the way it is! She made her choice and so have you. Christ, I should think you'd be the last one to question this shit. What did you think was going to happen? She'd be taken away in a white light? She's dead! She's been dead for weeks.

CHARLIE: Just...shut up. Right now. Ah-ah! Right now. Not a word. Not a fucking word.

            Enter DANA.

DANA: What's going on?

You mean I went all the way upstairs and back for nothing? …shit.

Ah, well, it's kinda' chilly down here, anyway.

> *DANA wraps herself in the blanket and sits on the end of the couch opposite SERA's body.*

A suicide that lasted a month and a half…Way to go, Sera.

Hey, isn't it cool that she survived until tonight? I mean, talk about timing!

Y'know…this whole thing would make a pretty good movie. It's got a real dramatic context goin' on.

CHARLIE: I should see about Tobi.

SAM: Hey. Mr Angry Poet. How about you play the role of the concerned guy after we get the body out of the rec room? It's kind of in the way, here.

CHARLIE: Uh…fine.

> *CHARLIE and SAM pick up SERA as DANA rails on. As soon as they leave the room, OCTOBER enters and DANA just keeps on yabbering to her.*

DANA: It was like what must have happened to that chick in *The English Patient*, only longer, 'cause Sera drank liquids, right? She, like, slowly died over six weeks. What a fuckin' cool suicide.

I wish I'd asked her what it was like… Y'know, to feel your organs shutting down and knowing there was nothing left for you but death? God this would make a good book. Sera had it down. That's what I'm talkin' about. Forethought, and dedication to the act. Sera's so cool.

This is gonna' be the best ever!

OCTOBER: I'm happy you're happy. Can I borrow your car?

DANA: My car? Why?

OCTOBER: I need to go for a drive…maybe get some beer.

DANA: I thought you were "flying dry".

OCTOBER: I'm not gonna' get smashed, I just wanna' get the
               edge off.

DANA: You're not gettin' uncool here, are you?

OCTOBER: Not by your standards, no.

               DANA gets up off the couch.

DANA: Explain that.

OCTOBER: I'm just saying, I…I'm cool.

DANA: You're cool.

OCTOBER: Yeah, I'm just feeling a little tense.

DANA: You're not like, thinking of backing out or nothing,
               are you? You're committed. You've made a
               commitment.

OCTOBER: I've got my trip right here.

               She pulls out the bottle of pills.

               I'm just gonna' lay down and sleep. It'll be cool.

               *DANA holds out her keys to OCTOBER.
               OCTOBER goes for a grab, but DANA pulls them
               out of reach.*

DANA: Cool?

OCTOBER: Cooler than yours.

DANA: What, you don't think hanging myself will freak the
               shit out of the person who finds me? I mean, c'mon,
               it's classic!

OCTOBER: Exactly. Classic; stodgy. Same difference. I should think a suicide connoisseur like yourself would come up with something a little more original. I mean, come on, Dana. It's been done.

DANA drops the keys into OCTOBER's hand.

DANA: Fuck you.

OCTOBER: Yeah, whatever.

> *OCTOBER leaves and DANA sits down on the couch as CHARLIE and SAM enter.*

SAM: I'm just saying...it's not like she'd mind. We're gonna' have to anyway, to put her in the sheet.

CHARLIE: Was that October?

DANA: Yeah.

CHARLIE: I swear to God, Sam, don't you touch her. I don't know what's going on with you, but you're changing by the minute. That's fuckin' sick, Sam. *Do not touch her.*

> *Exit CHARLIE.*

SAM: *(At CHARLIE.)* She told us to!

DANA: What was that about?

SAM: Well, I just figured we should probably take her clothes off and put her in that black sheet like she said. ...I guess Charlie took offense.

DANA: He can be a real dick.

SAM: I've noticed.

DANA: Charlie's romantic about death, yeah, but he doesn't understand how...How erotic it can be. It's very liberating.

> *DANA stands and approaches SAM.*

...peeling off her clothes...she doesn't care.

Running your hands over her skin...she doesn't care.

SAM: Dana...

DANA: You wanted her...when she was alive.

SAM: What?

DANA: You wanted to fuck Sera.

SAM: I did not!

DANA: Tsk tsk tsk. Did too.

You lusted for her. And all it was about was her body.

You couldn't admit deep down inside that while Charlie loves October for her soul, and he loved Sera for her innocence, the only thing you wanted from her was her flesh. Reality sucks, huh? Even the word itself is sharp. Painful to the ear. There's a term for it. "Cacophonic", I think. Fuck.

Fuckfuckfuckfuckfuck.

SAM: Quit it, Dana.

DANA: And you're too...disciplined to admit it. You won't admit you're that...shallow. That asshole you've trained yourself not to be.

And now...she's dead. She'll never be anything more. Her body's not even cold.

And now, Sam...you can strip her down, like you wanted to...touch her where she never would have let you before...

Like...here.

She points to her body.

Or maybe here.

SAM: I'm not fuckin' with you Dana, quit it!

DANA: You've probably got a hard-on right now just thinking about it....maybe even just thinking about me.

            DANA reaches out and caresses SAM's hair.

            ...poor Sammy. Such discipline. Such control. Why don't you ever let go? Go ahead. Say it.

SAM: What?

DANA: You want me. Right now. Don't you?

SAM: You're out of your mind.

DANA: You were right before...it's the end of the world. Why not indulge yourself? No one will know. No one will care.

            Any fantasy you've ever had, Sam. Go ahead. Violate me. I'll be dead in a few hours, and I think I've reached the point where I'm truly at terms with the fact that nothing I do right now matters.

            Even fucking a loser like you.

            SAM slowly reaches out and touches her cheek.

SAM: ...I don't even like you much.

DANA: And I think you're an anal retentive momma's boy asshole.

            She kisses him hard. SAM doesn't pull away.

            I think the contrast creates some nice sparks.

            DANA takes two fingers and points to the hollow at the base of her neck.

            Kiss it.

SAM: Dana, this...

DANA kisses him again, and leans back.

DANA: And if you feel the urge, use a little tongue.

"Come Rain or Come Shine" by Billie Holiday plays softly as they talk.

It's our last day on Earth, Sam.

She touches his lips.

And you're so beautiful.

She leans her neck back.

Go ahead.

The music jumps up a few decibels. SAM leans in and kisses her neck. He holds her to him, and she does the same as the lights fade to black. The music stays for the lines "I'm gonna' love you like nobody's loved you / come rain or come shine/ high as a mountain and deep as a river / come rain or come shine / I guess when you met me / it was just one of those things."

The lights come up on the steps. OCTOBER's sitting there, and CHARLIE enters.

CHARLIE: What're you thinking?

Pause.

OCTOBER: I'm thinking about Sera. It feels...I feel so awful...don't you?

CHARLIE: This was not the right thing for Sera. I know that now. She was better than this. She could have been anything.

OCTOBER: If it's not right for her, does that mean it's not right for me? Does that mean it's not right for you?

CHARLIE: No. No, you and Sera are dying to run away from something. I'm going towards it. I'm different.

OCTOBER: You are not.

CHARLIE: Tobi, don't do this.

OCTOBER: If you loved me, we wouldn't be having this conversation.

CHARLIE: Tobi... This has nothing to do with you. Nothing. This is...it's like us dating for the two weeks before one of us moves to Denver.

OCTOBER: Jesus Charlie!

               One; do not compare our relationship to "just dating." You and I, I'm sorry to burst your bubble, transcend a pair of kids hanging around, watching movies and fucking for two weeks.

               You and I have a genuine, real, nonfiction spiritual connection. You know we do. Two; "moving to Denver" is the worst suicide analogy ever. I mean *ever*.

               I've...never met anyone who loves life as much as you do. You run outside when it rains just to feel it on your face. How can you say you want to stop?

CHARLIE: It's not that I want to stop! It's that I want more. There are four experiences that are one hundred percent, perfect tens on the experience scale—birth, true love, the loss of that love, and death. And I want to know what the last two are like. I want to...know that.

OCTOBER: You're raping life. Hasn't it occurred to you that by forcing these experiences they won't be as real?

               You said my suicide was cheap-ass well God, Charlie.

               You're doing exactly what I was doing. You're just rationalizing it with intellectual bullshit.

               And it is bullshit, Charlie. It's complete bullshit. It's this fantasy fucking world you've created after living through whatever happened to you—

CHARLIE: Quit it.

OCTOBER: —that summer!

CHARLIE: Shut up! You have no clue!

OCTOBER: Then tell me! Because this romance shit of yours isn't real!

CHARLIE: *(roars)* Fuck! Just…. stop it.

             CHARLIE lights a cigarette. A long pause.

             Nothing happened. Nothing. I didn't have some life-altering near-death experience, I wasn't abducted or anything. Do you believe me?

             Pause.

             I just…things were going really bad for me. Things were really sucking. I was… Well, I was a complete asshole. And you know whose fault it was?

OCTOBER: Foster parents?

CHARLIE: Mine. Nobody molded me into being a drunk. Nobody sat me down and brainwashed me into being a car thief. It was me. I. Me. And I realized…what the fuck am I worth? This is it, this is me. And I am…I was the guy you were afraid of in dark alleys. I was the guy who mugs your best friend. I was the guy who steals your car.

             And so…I went off all ready to…I had a .22 rifle. I was gonna' just blow my head right off.

OCTOBER: Why didn't you?

CHARLIE: We need to get back inside.

OCTOBER: Why? What the fuck, Charlie! Why can't we just run? Away from all this shit! This whole thing is so stupid!

CHARLIE: I promised Sera I'd keep Sam's hands off her.

OCTOBER: As if Sam would—

            CHARLIE stands.

CHARLIE: He was trying to strip her down when I left.

OCTOBER: And you *left?*

            OCTOBER stands.

CHARLIE: I had to make sure you were okay.

OCTOBER: Jesus, Charlie.

CHARLIE: Let's just get back inside.

            *"Blues Before Sunrise" by John Lee Hooker plays.
            Exit CHARLIE and OCTOBER as the lights go
            down. Music plays for the lines "Blue before sunrise
            / the tears in my eye / blue before sunrise / with tears
            standing in my eyes / it's a horrible feeling / Lord
            knows I do despise" Lights come up on the empty rec
            room. Enter CHARLIE and OCTOBER.*

            (Offstage.) Daaaaaaanaaaa!!! Sam?

CHARLIE: Maybe they stepped out for a bit.

OCTOBER: Check on Sera.

CHARLIE: Yeah.

OCTOBER: You guys? Hello? They could've at least left us a
            note.

            Enter SAM, pulling on his shirt.

SAM: Hey October.

            *Enter DANA, her hair all disheveled and shirt a little
            undone.*

            Pause.

OCTOBER: Oh, you can't be serious.

CHARLIE: Well what the fuck.

SAM: Nothing happened!

DANA: Sam, you're such a pussy! As if it matters!

               DANA goes and sits on the couch.

CHARLIE: Ohhhh Sam.

SAM: Don't you even start. Dana's right. Nothing we do
               matters. Now that I'm dead, I can let go and start to
               live.

CHARLIE: That has *got* to be the most pathetic thing I've ever
               heard.

DANA: Let's just do this. You ready?

OCTOBER: What?

DANA: Your pills. Are you ready to go?

OCTOBER: Uh…yeah, I guess…just not right now.

DANA: Why not? It's like…almost four already. We have
               got to get moving on this! C'mon, Sera got the ball
               rolling, we need to pick up the pace! How do you
               want your body placed?

OCTOBER: I just want to take the pills and have my body be
               found where I hit the floor.

DANA: Oh…that's cool. Sam?

SAM: Same. Charlie, you ready?

CHARLIE: Jesus, I need a cigarette.

               CHARLIE lights a cigarette.

               Alright, let's do this.

SAM: Right.

               SAM kneels and pulls out his short blade.

CHARLIE: What're you doing? If you think I'm dragging your gutted body into the next room, then coming back for your head, you're out of your mind. This is a hundred and fifty dollar shirt. I'm not getting your blood on it.

SAM: Then take it off.

CHARLIE: Excuse me!

I chop off your head, *I* choose where we do it. Next room!

SAM gets up and picks up his duffel bag and goes into DANA's room.

SAM: Jesus. You can be such an ass…

CHARLIE: Oh, gimmie that sword.

By this time they're both gone.

OCTOBER: Dana…

DANA: Shh! I want to hear this.

OCTOBER: Hear what?

Pause.

Hear what?

SAM: (*Offstage.*) Aaaaaaaaauuuuuuuugggggghhhhhhh!!!! Jesus!! Jesus Christ, kill me! Fuck!! Charlie?! What the fuck!?

Enter CHARLIE, carrying the sword, looking a might pale. SAM continues to scream his head off.

DANA: Charlie, what the fuck?! What are you doing, he's still alive!

SAM's screams continue.

CHARLIE: No, fuck this! Fuck him, no way! I am *not* doing this!

DANA: You pussy fucking— Gimmie that!

                 *DANA takes the sword and goes into her room. We
                 hear a distinctive "thump".*

CHARLIE: Oh my God oh my God. This is so unhealthy.

                 Enter DANA, bloody sword in hand.

DANA: Well what the funny fuck! That was at least fifteen
                 seconds you let him live, there, Charlie! What the
                 hell happened to you? You used to have a stomach
                 for this!

CHARLIE: That was before my ex died on your sofa and my
                 friend asked me to chop off his head. Back off, Dana.

DANA: *(Composing herself.)* Well…The point is, he's dead.
                 No harm done, I guess.

OCTOBER: God…how much blood was there?

DANA: Oh…hey… Wanna come look?

                 OCTOBER and CHARLIE shake their heads.

                 I *can't* not. I'll be right back.

                 Exit DANA.

OCTOBER: Charlie…Charlie Jesus, I want to get out of here.
                 Let's go. Let's just fucking go! This is insane. We've
                 gotta' go.

CHARLIE: Tobi…

OCTOBER: Let's just get out of here right now. We'll go. We'll
                 go away. We'll drive until we hit an ocean. We'll
                 spend another two weeks together and if you still
                 feel the same way just break up with me and you
                 can… Let's just go.

CHARLIE: It's a pact, October.

OCTOBER: I don't care about the pact! I don't care! I want to
                 fucking live!

Screw Dana, she's out of her *mind!* This is insane!

Enter DANA, carrying the sword.

DANA: You…You said you were cool.

OCTOBER: I lied. I'm very very uncool. I don't want any part in this. This is sick, Dana. You're crazy, you need help.

DANA: You… *I'm* crazy…and you're the one firing insults at a girl with a giant butcher knife. Do I scare you?

OCTOBER: Put it down.

DANA: Do I scare you, Charlie? You're the only one who ever understood. Do I scare you?

CHARLIE: What are you going to do, Dana, you gonna' kill her? What is that worth? You wouldn't be a Suicide Queen, you'd just be that psycho girl. She has to choose to die, or it's not suicide. Those were your rules, remember? The pact is broken. You can't fix it.

Pause. DANA thinks over CHARLIE's spiel.

DANA: October…I had a very specific plan, here… This is a new art form. Can you appreciate that?

OCTOBER: Fuck your art form. Fuck you. I'm gonna' live.

DANA: You *bitch!* You fucking *bitch!* I trusted you! You are a piece of the puzzle! This whole thing…is *nothing* without you. Tobi…it was supposed to *wake people up.*

OCTOBER: Stop fucking with us! Do you think you're a rebel? Do you actually think you're a rebel? You're not a rebel! You are fucking psychotic!

DANA: You say tomayto, I say tomahto.

OCTOBER: Charlie, let's go. I wanna' get out of here.

DANA: You two are such a pair of codependent *fucks!* Fine. You won't kill yourself, and I can't make you. But my life will *be* something! Whenever someone even mentions the name "Dana" in Winnipeg, people will get goosebumps! They'll remember me! They'll think of the chick who smashed status quo social bullshit right in the face!

And no one will ever know you existed. Except maybe as the pussy who couldn't hack it.

And you, Charlie! Charlie! My inspired romantic. I have no clue what she does for you. But imagine what you're missing.

DANA pulls out a razor blade and slowly advances on CHARLIE, running it up his shirt.

Imagine… Watching your life spill out onto the floor. Feeling it drain away, and…

As DANA says "Whoah" she grabs CHARLIE's hair and keeps their faces within inches.

…whoah! …what a rush. And what is it, Charlie? What am I going to know in ten minutes that you won't? What will I see? Maybe I'll shake hands with the Devil. Maybe I'll learn the meaning of life. Maybe…I'll know everything. Maybe it'll be like every feeling of love and every feeling of hate and lust and pain and anguish and passion all at once…and you can't tell me that your heart isn't beating a little faster right now just thinking about it.

I'm gonna' go in there now, Charlie. And I'm gonna' find out.

She places the razor in CHARLIE's palm.

…I'll tell Sera you said hi.

DANA goes to leave and stops halfway.

…No…you'll tell her yourself. Won't you, Charlie?

Exit DANA.

OCTOBER: Ugh let's go!

CHARLIE: I can't.

OCTOBER: Don't tell me you're still gonna' do this!

CHARLIE: Tobi...

OCTOBER: No! No, you dumb bastard! You think Dana's right? This is a solution to nothing! This has all the romance of in vitro!

If you do this, you'll become nothing! Nothing! You will die and there will be nothing and you will be forgotten! You are worth more than that! You, here, alive, has worth! Can't you see that?

I actually thought you were cool, how can you be so stupid?

CHARLIE: All I was gonna' say was... Go outside. Wait for me. I'll be about five minutes. Dana told me to make sure her hair was decent, I need to make sure Sam's head is close to his body and I've got to wrap Sera in that sheet. I said I would and I will. Alright?

OCTOBER: Really?

CHARLIE: Yes.

OCTOBER: We're going?

CHARLIE: Yes.

OCTOBER: I'll...I'll be outside.

CHARLIE: Okay.

CHARLIE starts to go, but stops...

October?

OCTOBER: *(Turning.)* Yeah?

CHARLIE turns and walks back to OCTOBER. He kisses her very softly.

CHARLIE: I love you.

OCTOBER: I love you, too.

CHARLIE: I'll be five minutes.

OCTOBER: Okay.

Exit CHARLIE. OCTOBER goes out onto the steps.

I'm still scared.

I'm not scared that I made the wrong decision. I…I'm scared just…about my life. I'm scared like I was before I went suicidal, I guess. Life is scary. It's scarier than death, anyway.

Death isn't scary. Death is simple. Death is complete and comforting. It's a constant. A warm, inviting, calm blue.

She lights a cigarette.

Life is…fucking terrifying. Life's complex and stressful and dynamic… It blows your mind how complex. It blows my mind.

But…y'know…just knowing that I'm going to live it with someone kinda'…I suddenly see why Charlie loves heavy rains so much. Why he loves to just stand there and feel it on his face. All it is is…soaking up all the beauty. Because life is…the most romantic thing…

She takes a drag.

And I want to. Yes. I do. I want to live.

I don't know when that went away. I was born to live. Dana was born to die. And that…that was her goal.

This whole...this whole stupid thing was just a...just like a wrong turn, you know? Just a...just a bad little stretch of road. I am who I was before all this shit. But now I know why.

I thought I was seeing things clearly, like I was being more honest with myself, but...I haven't changed. I thought I had, but no. People don't change. Charlie was wrong. You can't...you can't change who you are. You can pretend...you can act. But who you really are, if you're someone who was born to live...that doesn't change.

And Charlie...

Charlie.

Her eyes pop open—it suddenly occurs to her. She stomps out the cigarette and turns back into the house. The lights go down on the steps and come up on the rec room. Enter OCTOBER.

Charlie!!

"Stormy Weather" by Billie Holiday plays.

Lights go down.

The End.

Author Biographies

Joseph Aragon is a Winnipeg playwright. He has been heavily involved in the Winnipeg Fringe Theatre Festival since 1999, as writer (*Swift Current*, 1999; *The Book of Changes*, 2000), performer, and musical director of 2001's hit horror spoof, *Sorority Girls Slumber Party Massacre: The Musical*. In 2003, his comedy *The Unlikely Sainthood of Madeline McKay* won the Harry S. Rintoul Memorial Award for Best New Manitoban Play at the Winnipeg Fringe Festival. *To Forgive, Divine* was featured in the *Spotlight Alberta and Beyond* showcase at the 2003 National *playRites* Festival in Calgary, and read as part of the *Under Consideration* reading series for Theatre Projects Manitoba. He currently studies playwriting at the National Theatre School of Canada in Montreal.

Ginny Collins is a playwright/journalist who lives in Winnipeg. In fourth grade she wrote a skit involving a globe and a tape deck and never looked back. Her other playwriting credits include *A Fine Christian Woman* and *Enter Captain Rogue*, the latter co-written with the members of the Where's Bobby collective. Ginny is currently sitting in her basement agonizing over what to call her third play involving World War I flying aces and UFOs. She is in the process of completing her degree in journalism and is now pretty hooked on this playwriting thing. If the other options don't work out then she has decided to become a poet, because that's where the real money is.

Rose Condo is a graduate of the Honours Theatre Program at the University of Winnipeg. *pyg* is her first play. Rose performed *pyg* at the 2003 Winnipeg and Edmonton Fringe Festivals. She has been known to act in and direct independent theatre productions, and can often be found teaching creative drama. She currently lives in Edinburgh, and she is not particularly fond of cats.

David Ferber started telling stories before he learned to write. He was born in Calgary, but has long considered Winnipeg his home. He is a regular contributor to CBC Radio, and is currently working on his first novel.

Primrose Madayag Knazan is most known for her successful plays *Spin* and *Shades of Brown*. She was co-writer for the River's Edge production of *Chutney, Kraft Dinner and Eggrolls* and was part of Sarasvati's "Femfest: a festival for women playwrights" with *Wallflowers & Wildflowers*. She has received several acclamations for her work, including grants from the Manitoba Arts Council and the Winnipeg Arts Council and was featured as an emerging playwright at the Winnipeg International Writers Festival. Primrose would like to thank the Manitoba Association of Playwrights for their dedication to developing playwrights and her husband Josh, for his love, support and patience.

About the Editor

Brian Drader is an actor, writer and dramaturge who makes his home in Winnipeg, Manitoba. As an actor, he has performed in over 70 professional stage productions, and numerous television and film projects.

As a writer, his plays include *Mind Of the Iguana* and *Easter Eggs* (both written with Stephen McIntyre), *The Fruit Machine, Tucktuck, Bubba and the Peter Eater, S*IT, The Norbals* (winner of the Herman Voaden National Playwrighting Competition, and premiering at Prairie Theatre Exchange in Winnipeg and The Canadian Stage Company in Toronto in '98), *Prok* (premiering at Theatre Projects Manitoba, winner of the Brick Playhouse New Play Award, Philadelphia, and nominated for the 2003 Governor General's Award, and the 2004 Lambda Literary Award, Drama, and the Manitoba Book of the Year Award), and *Liar* (finalist, the Joyce Dutka Arts Foundation Playwrighting Competition, New York).

The Norbals, Prok and *Liar* have all been published by Scirocco Drama.

As a screenwriter, his feature film *Alpha Woo* is in development with Ocular Productions. He won the National Screen Institute Drama Prize for his short film, *Iris and Nathan*, directed by Arlea Ashcroft, and produced by Teena Timm.